# Understanding Transgender Diversity

## A Sensible Explanation of Sexual and Gender Identities

# Understanding Transgender Diversity

## A Sensible Explanation of Sexual and Gender Identities

## Claire Ruth Winter

Front Cover Design: Shane Winter
Front Cover Concept and Photography: Claire Winter

Back Cover Concept: Ken Irish and Claire Winter
Back Cover Photography: Claire Winter

All diagrams: Claire Winter

LEGAL DISCLAIMER: This book is presented for informational purpose only, and is not intended to be a substitute for professional mental, medical or legal advice. Neither the author nor the publisher will be liable for any damages or harm that may result from any decision made or action taken due to any statement or interpretation of any information in this book. Please see Disclaimer section on page 7 of this book in the section entitled *The requisite disclaimer.*

ISBN: 1-45631-490-4

EAN-13: 978-1-45631-490-3

Published November 2010

© 2010 Claire Ruth Winter

All rights reserved. No part of this publication may be reproduced, stored in a retrieval system, or transmitted in any form or by any means, electronic, mechanical, photocopying, recording or otherwise, without the prior written permission of the publishers and/or author.

While every precaution has been taken in the preparation of this book, the publisher assumes no responsibilities for errors or omission, or for damages resulting from the use of information contained herein.

*To the gender pioneers of the 20th century, whose unquenchable passion to live integrity out loud accelerated an inexorable movement toward a most critical human right: to be openly true to yourself.*

*And to my son Shane,
whose true love endured great change,
whom I cherish with all my heart.*

**sen•sible** *adj* . . . **5** having appreciation or understanding; emotionally or intellectually aware **6** having or showing good sense or sound judgment; intelligent; reasonable; wise

—Webster's New World College Dictionary, Fourth Edition, Wiley Publishing, Inc., 2007, p. 1306.

# Contents

| | |
|---|---|
| **Acknowledgments** | 2 |
| **First Things First** | 4 |
| **I. The Diversity of Human Sexuality** | 11 |
| Let's Be Perfectly Clear About This | 12 |
| Human Sexuality: Why Transgender People Exist | 25 |
| On the Outside: Social Identity | 31 |
| On the Inside: Core Identity | 37 |
| Person to Person: Relational Identity | 48 |
| The Whole Picture | 54 |
| **II. The Spectrum of Transgender Expression** | 59 |
| Transgender Self-discovery | 60 |
| Responding to the Core | 67 |
| The Diversity of Transgender Identities | 71 |
| Changes to Physiology | 88 |
| **III. Relating to Diversity** | 95 |
| Accepting A Transgender Truth | 96 |
| Relational Shockwaves | 99 |
| The Family | 106 |
| Intimate Partners | 109 |
| Transgender Disclosure to Children | 120 |
| If Your Child Might Be Transgender | 124 |
| Friends and Relatives | 130 |
| Co-workers | 133 |
| Changes, Threats and Opportunities | 140 |
| Human Diversity, Human Rights | 145 |
| **Notes and References** | 161 |
| **Glossary of Transgender Terminology** | 167 |
| **About the Author** | 185 |

# Acknowledgements

So many wonderful people have contributed in countless ways to the content of this book, both directly and indirectly, that it's difficult to narrow it down to a surely incomplete list.

I am indebted to authors Chris Bohjalian, Kate Bornstein, Jenny Boylan, Leo Buscaglia, Jeffrey Eugenides, Anne Fausto-Sterling, Jamison Green, Arlene Istar Lev, Jan Morrison, Donna Rose, Lannie Rose, Joan Roughgarden, Julia Serano, Max Valerio, and many other writers whose perspectives and insights contributed significantly to my interpretations of the complex and controversial topic of human sexuality.

I owe a very special thanks to Arlene Lev, author of the landmark book "Transgender Emergence", both for the affirmation of her book's expansive content and for her gracious willingness to give me feedback while I formulated the models I present in this book. Likewise special thanks to Dr. Amy Ware for her very valuable perspectives and input.

So much of this book has been made possible by the years of enlightening interaction with my close friends. To my near-lifelong friend Ken Irish I can't begin to express my appreciation; his perspectives and commentary contributed most significantly to the final manuscript. Likewise my deepest thanks to Terrie Irish, Aiden Irish and Diane Dickey for their invaluable insights and steadfast love.

I could never sufficiently thank my dear friends and co-educators Meredith Bacon, Marsha Botzer, Shelly Cohen, Morgan Girling, Dee Graham, Ann Grogan, Andrea James, Mara Keisling, Aidan Key, Roberta-Ann Klitgaard, Nicole Kucera, Audrey Lamoureux, Elaine

# Acknowledgements

Lerner, Deirdre O'Callahan, Donna Rose, Karen Williams, and many others (you know who you are) for their input and insight—ranging from psychology to sociology to spirituality to friendship and love.

Nor could I ever sufficiently thank Dr. Douglas Ousterhout for his consummate skill: without him my new life and this book would literally not have been possible. The pictures on this book's final page show my gratitude much better than words. Likewise my heartfelt thanks to dear friends and sisters Mira Coluccio, Tatiana, Tricia and Mary Lou: so many of us have been re-born into the care of this wonderful "family."

I'm very privileged to extend my heartfelt gratitude to the faculty and students at my alma mater, Whitman College, with very special thanks to Anthropology Professors Suzanne Morrissey, PhD, and Jason Pribilsky, PhD, for their invaluable time and input, as well as that of Gender Studies Director Melissa Wilcox. I'm indebted to their respective anthropology and gender studies students for their insightful feedback—especially that of Ms. Katelyn Sorensen—that led to a much improved set of diagrams.

My thanks also to Dr. Manivong Ratts and Dr. Chris Wood of Seattle University and Dr. Peter Shalit of the University of Washington Medical School for inviting me to present and interact with their dedicated graduate and undergraduate students, to Dr. Michele Manber of Highline Community College for her valuable input, and to Dr. Howard Leonard for his wisdom and support.

My warmest thanks to Holly Boswell, Wendy Parker and Nancy Nangeroni for their contribution of the transgender symbol ⚧ that I have used liberally throughout this book.

Lastly and importantly I am deeply thankful for my son Shane. His steadfast love, artistic talents and human insights are of incalculable value to me. We are not only of the same flesh and blood, but are also the best of friends, a gift beyond value to any parent, and most certainly to this grateful author.

# First Things First:

## the Why, What and How of This Book.

**Why.** I wrote *Understanding Transgender Diversity* to respond clearly and compassionately to a most fundamental question that people ask when they initially encounter a "transgender" situation firsthand. And that question is basically this:

**"Would someone *please* explain to me, in plain English, what this 'transgender' thing is all about?!?"**

Although there is a great deal of transgender literature available, made ever more accessible via the internet, I realized early in my own gender transition that there wasn't a book available—that I could give to friends, family and co-workers—that specifically responded to this appropriate question with a *concise and understandable introductory presentation of the fundamentals*.

And that's where this book comes in.

Considering the controversial and sometimes stressful nature of a transgender announcement, I felt strongly that the first educational book one chooses to tackle should possess three important qualities that to date no other book has provided. I believe that an effective introductory book should be:

**1) Relatively short.** A transgender announcement quite often catches family, friends and co-workers off-guard, so there is usually an element of urgency to one's need to get up to speed on this controversial topic. Few people are willing to dive into a 350 to 500 page technical or memoir-based book in response to some very pressing questions; we want some concise answers right *now*.

So this book is intentionally short and to the point (a challenging task considering the subject). It will take you about the same amount of time to make a goodly dent in this book as it would to watch a re-run TV movie with way too many commercials. Yet in this time you will be amazed at what you can learn about the vast diversity of human sexuality that our culture has long been in deep denial to discuss openly.

**2) Visually clear and well-organized.** We humans are very visual creatures, not strictly verbal. In my interaction with many people over the years—from children to college students to seniors—I confirmed that visual diagrams can be highly effective in helping people to actually *see* patterns and connections in systems that might otherwise be difficult to grasp. So a lot of effort went into creating the pictorial diagrams in this book, and I think you will find them particularly helpful.

The information in this book is not new—very little under the sun is! It is the way in which human identity and sexuality is *presented and organized* that gives us an opportunity to see how much sense this all really makes. It is the social discomfort in which sexual topics have long been shrouded that has made things like being transgender more difficult to understand, because it's not socially accessible.

**3) Personable and easy to read.** While I could present the theories and models of human sexuality herein with a densely worded and somewhat academic presentation (*notwithstanding the overlying implications of conflated paradigms*), I much prefer a more casual and intimate form of conversation. As an educator I have personally experienced time after time that learning can be— even *should* be—enjoyable and vitalizing, not exclusively onerous, and I hope you will think so too while you read this book.

Furthermore, a positive attitude and a good sense of humor are values very near and dear to me. In fact I feel that these qualities— along with opposable thumbs—are important distinctions that separate human beings from the rest of the critters on this planet. It is in my nature to approach everything in a personable way, so my sense of humor sneaks in here and there throughout this book (*in parenthetical italics, such as in the preceding paragraph*). It is my hope that these quips make your reading experience as enjoyable as possible while not detracting from the importance of the material. More often than not these occasional comments are driven by compassion, which along with the content are dedicated to putting you more at ease in the face of significant change.

**What.** Although this book focuses primarily on transgender identity, it is ultimately about the *individuality of human beings*. ***It is a brief presentation of the fascinating relationship between our minds and bodies, how we see ourselves, and how we relate with others in our lives.*** And it explains how *the transgender experience is just one facet of the human experience, in all its natural diversity.*

This book concentrates on one of many obstacles we encounter in our effort to express our natural human diversity and individuality: in this case the culprit is ***sexism***. This is the underlying issue that leads to our need to even coin a word like "transgender."

We'll examine the degree to which sexism permeates our society and our many relationships, and how our physical genitalia are the bases for the sweeping, powerful social forces that start from the day we're born.

In many ways a lot of cultures actually work *against* individuality, for reasons some of which we'll discuss in Part III. It is this pervasive social pressure to *conform* that is so often the reason why certain kinds of diverse individuality—such as being transgender—have had to be hidden from public view.

**How.** Although the issues covered herein have been boiled down to the most basic forms I could determine, we are indeed complicated animals: so there's a *lot* of information packed into this diminutive book. Even something as simple as a bicycle can become

# First Things First

a bit overwhelming when you start taking it apart. So here's the rundown on a number of presentation features that should help you to digest this book most efficiently and enjoyably.

• **Part by part.** As you can see from the Contents page this book is divided into three Parts. These are arranged in an order "from the ground up," starting with the underlying psychology of human sexuality—why transgender people exist—moving on to an overview of transgender diversity, then finishing off with some insights on how to relate to the transgender people (and others) in your life.

You can, however, jump right into Part III for some urgent relational perspectives, or start off with Part II for a quick overview of transgender identities, and then at any time go back to Part I for the underlying psychology on which the subsequent sections are built. The book is laid out so that you can refer back to it easily for questions that might arise during or after your first read-through.

• **Time-saving tools.** Knowing that daily life is frantic enough as it is, I formatted this book with two handy tools to save you time.

1. Each section is labeled with a bold headline, so you can easily skim the pages, choose the topics that interest you and skip the rest if you want to.

2. Additionally, I've pulled out key phrases that summarize important points in most sections, each marked with a transgender symbol: ⚧. It's another quick way you can get the gist of the book without necessarily reading the fine print—although said fine print has much of interest to offer.

**The requisite disclaimer.** Before we dive headlong into enlightenment, I *must* stress that I am NOT a licensed therapist, psychologist or psychiatrist—but I *am* an experienced transgender person with a love for learning, a teaching degree, and a passion for educating about something of social and human importance. ***So do keep in mind that this presentation is but* one way *to look at the***

***very complex psychological topic of human sexuality.*** There are precious few universal absolutes in the highly intricate and organic science of human psychology, and I'm not claiming that this book is one of them. It is, though, a different *angle* on things, one that might shed a bit more light on the subject (thus the front and back cover designs).

I want to be very clear that though I suggest ways in which you might think about situations and prepare to deal with them, ***these are in no way intended as substitutes for qualified professional guidance***, as I point out many times, particularly in Part III. Rather I vehemently recommend that you ***obtain qualified professional advice before you take any action, and not rely solely on perspectives presented in this book***.

As I will describe later, I don't believe that transgender people are by definition burdened by an internal disorder. On the contrary it is *society's lack of tolerance* that results in disorders in a population that is simply responding to natural human diversity, a diversity that is replete in nature and inevitable in such complex organisms as human beings. And thus I think that *transgender people themselves will be instrumental in articulating the psychology and experience of this human phenomenon.*

**The larger perspective.** I hope that during the few hours that you spend reading through this book you are motivated to step back and think about the human perspectives I've tried to articulate, as a transgender person who realized I did not fit into my culture's sexist system and so stepped outside of it to take a long, hard look.

Other cultures in history have more officially recognized and valued the perspectives of transgender people, since we can observe the sexist operation of societies from the more objective position of standing outside of the established system. So it makes sense that the same can be done for Western cultures through the transgender people of today, and it's in this spirit that I offer this book.

The word "offer" above is very important. Again, I don't claim to present a declaration of absolute truths: the audacity of that is far beyond me. And I, for one, am deeply suspect of anyone who *does* preach a trunk-full of "incontrovertible" claims. Philosopher and mathematician Bertrand Russell once said, **"The whole problem with the world is that fools and fanatics are always so certain of themselves, but wiser people so full of doubts."**

I have also found, at least in my own life, that it is far more important to continually ask questions than to become complacent with pat answers. Unless we keep up an effort to continually probe with open minds, after all, we will never discover the best personal answers in a dynamic and constantly changing universe.

Nor do I feel that a questioning mind is incompatible with a trusting one: I find the mystery of the cosmos to be the source of both a deep faith and of endless fascinating questions. So it is my desire that this book will encourage you to likewise **consistently ask questions, with an open eagerness to learn and to grow from them**: that is a joy to which we humans have unique access.

This introductory book is a good place to *begin* a learning process that will help you to understand and benefit from a new kind of relationship with an old friend, a co-worker, a family member, a spouse or even yourself; with someone who has perhaps been haunted throughout life with an inner but socially unacceptable truth; with someone who has chosen, at great risk, to live with integrity, to be truly individual; with someone who is: transgender.

"... transgendered people embody some of humanity's greatest secrets."

—Arlene Istar Lev

# I.

# The Diversity of Human Sexuality

## Let's Be Perfectly Clear About This

For centuries many cultures have deemed it socially inappropriate to speak openly about most aspects of our "sexuality," a term commonly thought to refer exclusively to our physical sex characteristics and their somewhat embarrassing utilization. It's a taboo subject with which our Western society finds itself, ironically, quite obsessed.

Since the term "sexuality" bears the root word "sex" and all that it implies, it is socially laced with innuendo and ambiguity. There are many sexual terms with more or less the same meaning, others that are inaccurate, and many that are totally mysterious to many.

Before we can understand the meaning of "transgender," it is critical that we first clarify a number of basic terms and definitions, starting with the root word of much that this book covers: *sex*.

**The truth about "sex."** Like so many words in English, the term "sex" has a number of meanings, a serious shortfall of language that needlessly leads to so many problems (*how hard is to make up more words, already: even infants can do it*). So it's very important that we settle on the meaning of this fundamental term that's not only the most appropriate for our discussion on transgender issues, but one that reflects the biological truth regarding human beings.

Biologically speaking, an organism's sex classification is defined by the *gametes* it produces: males produce male gametes (spermatozoa) and females produce female gametes (ova). Rather than test each organism for it's gametes (*a dicey undertaking, to be sure*), we instead classify most creatures immediately according to their **visible reproductive organs,** or *genitalia*.

Outside the technical bounds of biology, however, gametes are out of the picture and the classification is based on *physiological* characteristics of the individual. After a comparison of about 10 different reference dictionaries, including medical, this is the definition that they pretty much all share:

**sex** *n.* a classification of male or female based on many criteria, among them reproductive, anatomic, and chromosomal characteristics.

Human beings have traditionally been assigned a sex at birth through visual examination of exterior genitalia (reproductive organs). More recently chemical samples from the womb can reveal the sex of the fetus before it is born.

This would seem pretty straightforward, as we've all assumed, but *there are two potentially serious flaws in the traditional means of assigning a person's sex*:

1. Visible examination of genitalia doesn't necessarily tell the whole story, nor are genitalia sufficiently consistent in size and shape to guarantee correct interpretation.

2. Nature doesn't adhere to our tidy assumption that there are only strictly male or female individuals.

The fact is:

▼ **People can be born naturally with both types of reproductive organs and/or chromosomal variations from strictly XX or XY and/or possess ambiguous genitalia that are not clearly male or female.**

People who are born neither exclusively male nor female are termed ***intersex***, and these births occur more often than most people realize. As we'll discuss later, there are national organizations that advocate for intersex folks, which is very important since these naturally born people can suffer both prejudice and mutilation without their consent.

So even though there are only two classes of sexual *organs*, male and female, when it comes to the *whole individual* it is a different story. As much as society does not want to recognize it, there are more than two "sexes."

The above facts are also why I will use the term "assigned sex," because that is what actually happens at birth: someone, usually a physician, *assigns* us as either male or female (in most cases) and this may or may not reflect the actual truth or the whole truth.

Though it might seem to you that dwelling on these technicalities delays our getting down to the transgender nitty gritty, it's precisely these kinds of fundamental misinterpretations and inaccuracies that lead to social discrimination and prejudice, of which being intersex and transgender are difficult ones. This is why it is so critical to agree on the meanings of many of these most basic terms.

**Sexism**. It's bad enough that most societies only recognize and allow two sexes, but it gets *much* worse: affecting much more than half the population. Instead of keeping sex strictly the physiological thing that it is, social structures have gone a serious step further by firmly expecting and restricting one's behavior, mental and physical capacities, and many fundamental rights based solely on that individual's assigned sex. The term for this is ***sexism***, and this widespread form of discrimination is one of the primary factors contributing to the very concept of "transgender" identities.

▼ **Sexism is defined as the unfair treatment, privilege or expectation of any person or group of people on the basis of their assigned sex.**

I think most would agree that our modern Western society has been distinctly divided, even made *divisive*, through widespread *sexism*: **how we function in many cultures is powerfully influenced by the sex that we are born into**.

# The Diversity of Human Sexuality

Although the term "sexism" is most commonly specified to feminist issues, for very good reason, I mean this term in an even broader sense in this book. Because social discrimination, prejudice, restrictions or expectations of any kind that are based primarily on one's sexual category are in fact potentially harmful to *any* sex.

Sexism is everywhere, woven so intricately into our language that we can't even distinguish much of it. We are nurtured and clipped and shaped by it, empowered and repressed by it, but in the end most *everyone* is *restricted* by it.

As we'll see in a moment, the very concept of a transgender identity is one result of sexism: that we expect people of a certain sex (physiology) to only behave in certain ways, within certain boundaries. And when we don't, we're in big social trouble.

**The meaning of "sexuality."** This is another important term that stems from the root word "sex." In order to understand how actually *logical* the transgender perspective really is (*I know what you might be thinking: bear with me on this one*), we need to "dissect" human *sexuality*: to identify all those things going on inside us and between us that are actually influenced by our anatomical sex.

Let's first confirm exactly what is meant by the root word "sexual," as our venerable Mr. Webster sees it:

**sexual** *adj.* 1. of, characteristic of, or involving sex, the sexes, the organs of sex and their functions, or the instincts, drives, behavior, etc. associated with sex.[1]

Based on this, our definition for *sexuality* will read:

▽ **Sexuality is an individual's total set of physical, mental and relational characteristics that are in any way influenced by that person's anatomical sex.**

Your personal sexuality is a very individual combination of all of the behaviors, instincts, physical characteristics and relational drives that are in any way influenced by your sex. Which is a *lot* but, with all due respect to Dr. Freud, nowhere near *everything*. All of these aspects of sexuality will vary from person to person and are therefore termed *variables*

So sexuality does not refer to our "sexiness"—the degree to which we flaunt our bodily topography. As you can see from the above this term has a much more encompassing meaning than most people usually give it.

**The difference between sex and gender.** Probably the most important distinction in definitions that we need to make, in order to talk accurately about sexuality, is the difference between the two fundamental terms *sex* and *gender*.

"Gender" has all too often been considered a synonym for "sex," both of these referring to our being male or female. You've undoubtedly filled out forms that ask you to indicate your:

Gender: ☐ Male   ☐ Female. (Answer: *neither*; read on.)

Even our faithful dictionary reflects the popular ambiguity regarding these terms.[1] Fear not, however: we transgender folks are here to settle this confusion once and for all. Here's what these terms should specifically mean, in order to keep things clear:

**Sex** *n.* The *anatomical* condition of being male, female, intersex, or neuter, as determined by genitalia and/or chromosomes.

**Gender** *n.* A psychological term for the nature of *behavioral* traits socially associated with each sex in a particular culture: masculine for males, feminine for females, androgynous for both and neuter for neither.[2]

So: "gender" is *not* really a synonym for "sex," as many people have believed—these two words are not interchangeable. There's little sense, after all, in having two different words with the same meaning, or worse yet a single word with several meanings.

*Sex* is of the *body* while *gender* is of the *mind*. To understand "transgender," we need to always keep these meanings distinct.

⚧ **A favorite expression among transgender people is, "Sex is between the legs, and gender is between the ears."**

It is very important to realize that **gender is a social construct**, an artificial division of a great many human personality characteristics into the two classes of masculine and feminine, expected to be consistent with one's anatomical sex.

**Gender is only a *portion* of the whole personality picture.** Any behavioral characteristics that are naturally or socially influenced by our anatomical sex *do not comprise the whole of our personality*.

⚧ **Gender is really a fundamentally sexist term for the *portion* of one's whole personality that is affected by our socially recognized sex.**

So it's important to realize that gender is but one facet of a person's whole and very complex personality, which encompasses a great many values, perspectives, interests, mannerisms and so on.

Our faithful mentor Webster offers this definition of personality (I've confined a rather long version to the most appropriate #3a):

**personality**, *n.*, 3 a) habitual patterns and qualities of behavior of any individual as expressed by physical and mental activities and attitudes; distinctive individual qualities of a person, considered collectively.[1]

It would be safe to say that a significant percentage, if not majority, of an individual's personality in fact has little to do with that person's sexuality. This is something to keep well in mind, as is reflected in the sexuality model and diagrams I offer in this book.

**The *binary* social view of gender.** Because so many societies only recognize two sexes—male and female—gender is viewed by these cultures as being *binary: either masculine or feminine*. By the term "binary" we mean that there are only two choices: black or white, right or wrong, male or female, masculine or feminine: *with no grey areas, no in-between, no other options.*

Furthermore the binary social view says that if you're male, you're confined strictly to one set of gender behavioral regulations: the *masculine* traits of being, strong, assertive, goal-oriented, competitive, showing little emotion and the like. If you're female, you have a completely different set of *feminine* gender requirements: being intuitive, nurturing, emotionally open, physically delicate, sensitive and so forth.

Gender expectations vary greatly based on geographical locale, era, ethnicity, group dynamics and other factors. And while you might think that all males and females conform to their social genders completely *naturally*, think again:

▽ **Gender characteristics are not all universal: many particular gender expectations are defined and conditioned into us by the local society in which we function.**

Try making a two-column list of masculine and feminine gender qualities at a gathering, with everyone contributing a trait. It's a very interesting exercise that will stimulate lots of conversation, if not controversy, demonstrating how truly vague yet intolerant the concept of gender can be (*indeed, "vague" and "intolerant" are not good bedfellows*). This exercise proves that specific qualities of gender not only vary from culture to culture, time to time, and locale to locale, but from *person* to *person* as well.

**Gender, sex-role and gender role.** Speaking of different terms with essentially the same meaning, here are two more. In your expansive gender research you are very likely to run across two other synonyms: *sex-role* and *gender role*. These all describe a set of behavioral characteristics that are socially associated with one's recognized sex.

I personally favor *sex-role* because it is particularly effective in stressing the role of sexism in social behavior. This term also sidesteps the confusion between *gender* and *sex* that we see everywhere. I find *gender-role* a tiny bit redundant: gender is a way we act, and a role is also something we act. *Sex-role* keeps the "sex" in these social roles (*easy now, you know what I really mean*), keeping it apparent in the language that gender is really a sexist view of personality. So I will most often use "sex-role" in this book, but will also use gender and gender role on occasion as valid alternate terms.

**Distinguishing between "male/female" and "man/woman."** Having endured the preceding diatribe on terminology, you're now prepared to realize the following important distinction between the terms **male/female** and the corresponding terms **man/woman**—a distinction not clearly understood by many of us (including me, not too long ago). *Male/female* refers of course to sexual anatomy, while *man/woman* refers to the expected social **sex-roles** of males and females, respectively (*"Ah-haaa," you say*).

⚧ **"Woman" is the social sex-role (or gender) of a female, and "man" is the sex-role of a male.**

This distinction is critical in understanding how transgender people view themselves and how they might want to be considered by others. They demonstrate that, to the surprise of many, you don't have to be a female to be a woman, or a male to be a man (*yes, the urge to close your eyes and pinch the bridge of your nose is quite appropriate at this point*).

**Feminine women and masculine men are our traditionally prescribed social sex-roles, that we popularly call genders.** And it has been socially unacceptable for anyone to step openly outside of these sex-role boundaries: a fact that lies at the root of such transgender manifestations as cross-dressing (as we'll see later).

Not only is there a distinction between our sex and our gender, but both of these are considered from a transgender perspective to be distinct and independent from our so-called *sexual orientation*: who we're physically attracted to (we'll talk more about sexual orientation further on).

**The independence of sex, gender and sexual orientation.** Many societies have traditionally held that our physical sex (assumed to be male or female, exclusively) doesn't just influence but rather *determines* both our gender (personality restrictions) *and* our sexual orientation (the sex we're attracted to). These three aspects of our sexuality have been historically locked together in many cultures, requiring that, for example, all males must be masculine *and* heterosexual and all females feminine *and* heterosexual.

The growing spectrum of studies and literature on sexual orientation and gender indicates that this social perspective does not correlate with sociological and scientific findings.[3] In other words, our historical sexually-determinative system is inconsistent with what is proving to be a natural human diversity, a diversity that underlies any socially or religiously applied morals and restrictions. These studies are showing that:

⚧ **Our gender and our sexual orientation are not strictly determined by our sexual anatomy.**

# The Diversity of Human Sexuality

This means that anyone can naturally possess *any combination* of the following options:
- **Sex**: male, female, intersex or neuter;
- **Gender**: masculine, feminine, both, or neither;
- **Sexual orientation**: hetero-, homo-, bi-, or asexual.

By the term "naturally" I mean that *there are both biological and psychological developments that occur in individuals prior to any social conditioning or other outside influences.* We'll talk about these in detail later on.

The fact that sexual orientation is a separate issue from gender is counter-intuitive for many people. It is why we are prone to expect a male who changes sex to female must also switch from being attracted to women to being attracted to men (as often couched by the question after a transgender announcement, "Does this mean you're gay?"). As we shall see further on,

▽ **Gender and sexual orientation are two separate issues involving completely different areas of the brain, so orientation may or may not be affected by a sex or gender change.**

We'll make some sense out of this potentially confusing issue further on in this section, so hold this thought.

**Now, at long last: the definition of "transgender."** (*Drum roll, please.*) Having hacked your way through the preceding to a relatively clear understanding of gender, sex and the binary nature of our prevailing social sex-role system, we are now able to define the specific meaning of "transgender."

The prefix "trans" means "across", and we now know what "gender" means. So the whole word means "across gender" or *crossing gender boundaries*. In other words:

⚥ **Anyone who regularly feels, acts or appears noticeably inconsistent with the social sex-role (gender) requirements of males and females is defined as transgender.**

Well *that's* not so complicated, is it? This covers a *lot* of people, though, when you really think about it. So it's a matter of *degree* that slips one into transgender territory.

Fear not, o techno-minded, here's a dictionary-style definition:

**Transgender** (*adj.*) *An umbrella term referring to any person who regularly feels and may consequently desire to act and/or appear significantly inconsistent with the social sex-role requirements established by the prevailing local culture.*

As that mouthful of a definition suggests, there is more than one avenue through which people can express a self-defined transgender identity. There are in fact three fundamental ways that a transgender identity can be expressed, through:

- **Personal appearance:** clothing and adornment, and/or
- **Behavior:** personality and mannerisms, and/or
- **Physical anatomy:** sex-specific bodily features.

The various combinations of these avenues loosely define some of the general transgender profiles that we will discuss in detail in Part II. Transgender is an *inclusive* term that covers a wide variety of gender expressions and sexual identities.

It's important to notice in the definition that ***being transgender is something you can feel within yourself—that you don't fit the sex-role that society requires of you—even if you don't express this in any way.*** If you do look or behave different enough from local sex-role requirements, others may consider you to be transgender even if you think you still fit your sex-role, stretched though it might be. In the end it should really be a matter of self-identity: ***being transgender is something that should be determined by that individual.***

**Gender variance is more involved in discrimination than we usually think.** An example of the way society associates gender and sexual orientation together lies in this anecdote. A male is walking along when a group of other males suspect him of being gay—even though they've never met him—and they begin to harass him. What is it that made them suspicious that he is gay?

Answer: in this case his feminine *gender*. The group assumed he was gay because they associated his effeminate mannerisms with homosexuality. So the truth is **this man was harassed because he was noticeably transgender.** Had his gender been masculine, as many gay males indeed are, he would not have been bothered. This anecdote demonstrates that transgender identity is much more involved in human diversity than one might think.

**Oppositional sexism.** There's one more term worth mentioning here. It's important to realize the revealing nature of the phrase "opposite sex" that we hear so often, and how it sets the stage for a transgender perspective. It indicates a widespread view that 1) there are only two sexes, and 2) these sexes are *completely opposite*.[4]

This drives home how extreme that binary thinking can become: that not only are the sexes considered so different in many ways, but that these differences have been so grossly exaggerated that males and females have virtually nothing in common and in fact "oppose" one another. It's a view that has, in spite of an increasing knowledge base to the contrary, degenerated to the point of *"Men Are From Mars, Women Are From Venus"* as expressed by the title of a popular book by Dr. John Gray[5] (intimating that men and women represent different species). As we will see, this is not only highly inaccurate but is actually discriminatory for people of any sex.

So instead of "opposite sex" I will use more appropriate phrases like *other sex-role* or *target sex*. There are occasions where I *will* use the phrase "opposite sex," with quotation marks, to point out this binary perspective. As we will see in following sections, **males and females have a lot more in common with each other than they have differences between them.**

**Planned obsolescence.** Ultimately the word "transgender" should become obsolete as we, as a society, understand the inherent *individuality* of human beings. Appropriate individual rights and freedoms become possible when we stop asking one another "***What*** are you?" and instead ask "***Who*** are you?" Male, female, masculine, feminine, transgender, transsexual, crossdresser, bisexual: these are all "*whats.*" Can we not instead open ourselves up to the uniqueness of human individuals? As we'll talk about later on, we have an unfortunate sociological obsession with *categories*.

**A convenient abbreviation.** To reduce the staggering number of times the term "transgender person" will come up from here forward, I'll often substitute it with the abbreviation **TG** instead—short for TransGender. In fact transgender people often refer to each other as "TGs" in somewhat the same spirit that WW II soldiers referred to one another as "GIs". Other times we refer to each other as "trans," short for the adjective transgender (e.g. "He's a trans friend of mine.").

Another abbreviation I will mention here, even though it doesn't come up all that much in this book, is **LGBT** (sometimes written as GLBT). It stands for Lesbian Gay Bisexual Transgender, and refers to the overall "non-binary" population, as I like to call it. More recently you will see the letter "Q" appended, which stands for Queer (that word has a new meaning: see *The Diversity of Transgender Identity* in Part II). So you will often see **LGBTQ** as well.

# Human Sexuality:
# Why Transgender People Exist

Transgender people have existed in many cultures throughout recorded history.[6] And we have to remember that history is written by the prevailing, so these reports are prone to be quite biased. We can only suspect that many societies chose not to recognize the existence of sexual-/gender-variant people in their midst. Moreover, the fact that transgender people have faced very real danger in revealing their presence greatly encourages them to refrain from doing so.

It's important to keep in mind this historical perspective on the existence of transgender people, so that we can better understand that the nature of human sexuality has not essentially changed or "degenerated"—as some would unfortunately consider it—in recent years. It is actually a matter of better research capabilities and the ability to make findings on social and psychological issues more available to the public: *that* is what's changed.

As one might suspect, the existence of the internet has been a significant factor in not only making important information widely and easily accessible, but *it has also allowed transgender people to better find and communicate with each other*. This is an important step in the process of socially marginalized groups (minorities) becoming organized, in order to affect social awareness and the kinds of societal and legal rights they ultimately deserve.

It would also be helpful, before we dive into sexual enlightenment, to step back and realize how truly *individual* in nature that human beings have always been, and how this fundamentally drives the diversity in human sexuality that we'll discuss in this book.

**No two human beings are exactly alike.** Not even identical twins: in fact there are several recorded cases of *identical twins* progressing to *different* gender and/or sexual identities (one changes sex and/or gender and the other does not).[7]

So it is critical to remember that ***humans are highly individual creatures***, due in large part to our incalculable physical and mental complexity. One of the most important messages of Part I in this book is to demonstrate the individuality of human beings, and that *a restrictive binary sex-role system works significantly against the ability for a great many people to live a fundamental civil right: integrity—being true to one's self.*

**One way to look at sexuality** is to consider that ***it is the individual product of many* independent *variables***—the key word being *independent*—that is, not locked strictly to one's genitalia. This is a perspective that, in various forms, is shared by many professionals; the model I present in this book is my own form of combining a number of these.[8]

If we can somehow boil all the complex diversity of human sexuality down into it's more basic "moving parts," then we might *start* to make some logical sense out of it all—and it's pretty basic human nature to want to make *sense* out of things, yes? So the model I present in this book is *one* (but certainly not the only) way to define a set of fundamental variables that, when assembled, form the uniquely personal sexuality that each of us possesses.

**First, we are creatures of mind and body.** Though our brains are indeed physiological organs in our bodies, most would agree that we as humans have *consciousness*: we are self-aware, we think, analyze, respond, rationalize, emote, communicate and interact with our *minds*—a word we often use instead of the anatomical word "brains." The mind is really the *operation* of the brain.

So in a sense there is a kind of mysterious distinction between this *cerebral* organ and the rest of the organs of our bodies. *This one's in charge*: it ultimately controls our entire being, and in turn is itself influenced by the body from which it receives constant signals (either consciously or subconsciously).

Whether this mind/body distinction is scientifically quantifiable or not, most would agree that we regard one another—and even our own selves—on two separate levels: one *mental* and the other *physical*. Although it can be hard to draw a sharp line between these two aspects of our being, I believe it will ultimately make things easier to understand if we each recognize the distinct roles that *mind* and *body* play in how we see and relate to ourselves and to others.

**"I can relate."** This consciousness that we humans possess winds up *interacting* with the world around us and within us. And of course interaction works both ways: that is, you relate to others and others relate to you. So when you step back and consider the ways you interact with your personal realities, they seem to fall into three fundamental categories:

- How society sees and relates to you;
- How you see and relate to yourself inside;
- How you see and relate to others individually.

Each of these relational avenues has a mental (behavioral) component to it and a physical component: people regard you from a mental standpoint and from a physical one, with your physical presentation often being the first and sometimes only thing people know about you (which is one basis for sexism). Likewise you see yourself and others as having minds and bodies, and to varying degrees you treat these separately.

So one way to look at sexuality is to define six fundamental ways (three pairs) in which you relate to your world. These are:

1-a) How society regards your behavior.
1-b) How society regards your physical appearance.
2-a) How you regard your inner self: your inner personality.
2-b) How you regard your own body.
3-a) How you regard different personalities around you.
3-b) How you regard different physical bodies around you.

We'll dissect these variables in great detail shortly, complete with pictures and arrows, but first we need to talk about an important underlying human concept: ***identity***. This term lies at the foundation of the six proposed factors of our sexuality, so let's explore this a bit.

**"May I see your identity, please?"** Well . . . that depends. The concept of *identity* is key in understanding the transgender perspective, but it's something a TG must be careful about revealing. And since we are never ones to leave things to chance, our next stop on the road to human enlightenment is the local library reference section.

>**identity**, *n.* **2** a) the condition or fact of being a specific person or thing; individuality[1]

As the definition suggests, identity is the set of recognizable characteristics—certainly physical but also ideological as well (ethnicity, religious faith, etc.)—that distinguish the individual "you" from "everyone else." Similarly it is how you distinguish *other* individuals among the sea of people you encounter in your life from day to day.

Central to our sexuality discussion, your identity is also a form of *consciousness*, your awareness of a self that is distinct from everyone around you. Human beings possess a degree of self-consciousness that separates us from the rest of the animals on spaceship earth (*at least as far as we know, dolphins and whales notwithstanding).*

Identifying is a more specific way of seeing: we don't just observe something, we *regard* it, *distinguish* it and are able to *recognize* it as something unique and memorable.

So all of these proposed sexuality variables involve *identity*: how others identify you, how you identify yourself, and how you identify others around you—each of these having a physical aspect and a mental one. Let's call each of these identity avenues by the following terms:

- How you are regarded by others: your ***Social Identity***;
- How you regard yourself deep inside: your ***Core Identity***;
- How you regard other individuals: your ***Relational Identity***.

| Social Identity | Core Identity | Relational Identity |
|---|---|---|
| How others regard you:<br>• mentally<br>• physically | How you regard yourself:<br>• mentally<br>• physically | How you regard others:<br>• mentally<br>• physically |

**Six Facets of Identity**

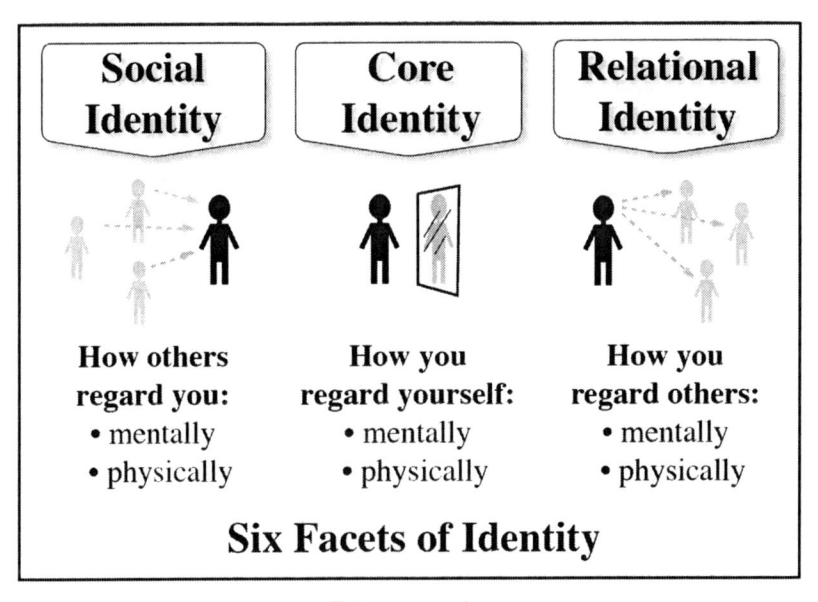

Diagram 1

Each of these facets of identity is comprised of a mental aspect and a physical one. Diagram 1 is a pictorial representation of these six variables of your overall identity.

As we'll talk about in more depth shortly, how you are seen by society is dependent on how you *present* yourself publicly, which may or may not be very consistent with who you really are inside.

Relational Identity is comprised of the types of attractions that we *identify with* or identify ourselves as *having*. And it's how we are identified or classified by *others* according to the type of attractions we display; that is, whether we are heterosexual, homosexual, bisexual (assuming there are only two sexes) or asexual. We'll talk about this in much greater depth a little further on in this section.

Diagram 1 is really a pictorial version of what mathematicians call a "matrix": in our sexuality model this would be the two aspects of mind and body interacting with each of the three facets of identity. A more scientific presentation of this sexuality matrix would look like the table in Diagram 2.

| Matrix: | Social Identity | Core Identity | Relational Identity |
|---|---|---|---|
| **Mind** | Outer Behavioral ID | Inner Mental ID | Attraction to minds |
| **Body** | Outer Physical ID | Inner Physical ID | Attraction to bodies |

Diagram 2: A Matrix Version of the Six Facets of Identity

So this approach to identity is one way of beginning to break down a complex answer to the question "Who do you consider yourself to be?" into distinct sexuality variables. Having this kind of clarity can help us to both ask ourselves enough of the right questions and to be better able to understand those around us.

Now we can delve more deeply into each of these distinct identities that combine to form a very unique sexuality for every individual.

# On the Outside: Social Identity

**How you are seen by society.** We each have a *Social Identity* in society. *It is how we present ourselves publicly*, how we are identified by the people around us from day to day. It's the one type of identity that's externally apparent about each of us. Often our public identity is a *compromise* between our real preferences (how we'd act and look if we had more social freedom to do so) and what is expected or demanded of us by some of the social mores of our local culture.

Although this book focuses on gender and sexual issues, we need to remember that, as pointed out earlier, *there is more to our outer and inner identities and values than sexuality*. So **these diagrams and models are by no means complete representations of human character**. Rather this is a way to break down the *sexuality* aspect of our being into fundamentals that we can distinguish.

Let's consider that there are two sexuality elements of your Social Identity: your **Apparent Gender** (the mental part: the portion of your personality affected by your sex) and your **Apparent Sex** (the physical part). The word "apparent" is important here, since what we *see* about someone doesn't always reflect the whole truth (as you may have recently discovered). And since a picture is worth a thousand head-scratches, these elements are shown graphically in Diagram 3. Go ahead and look it over, I'll wait . . . Okay, further explanation is in order.

**Distinguishing between mind and body.** Again, this distinction is key in understanding the complexity of human sexuality. The roles of mind and body are graphically portrayed in the diagram by the horizontal line of up/down arrows dividing the diagram into the upper

## Your Social Identity
### How others regard you.

**Society** | **You**

**Apparent Gender**
⟨Masc-Androg-Femn-Neut⟩
Sex-role part of personality

The sex-role part of your social personality and mannerisms that you choose to present

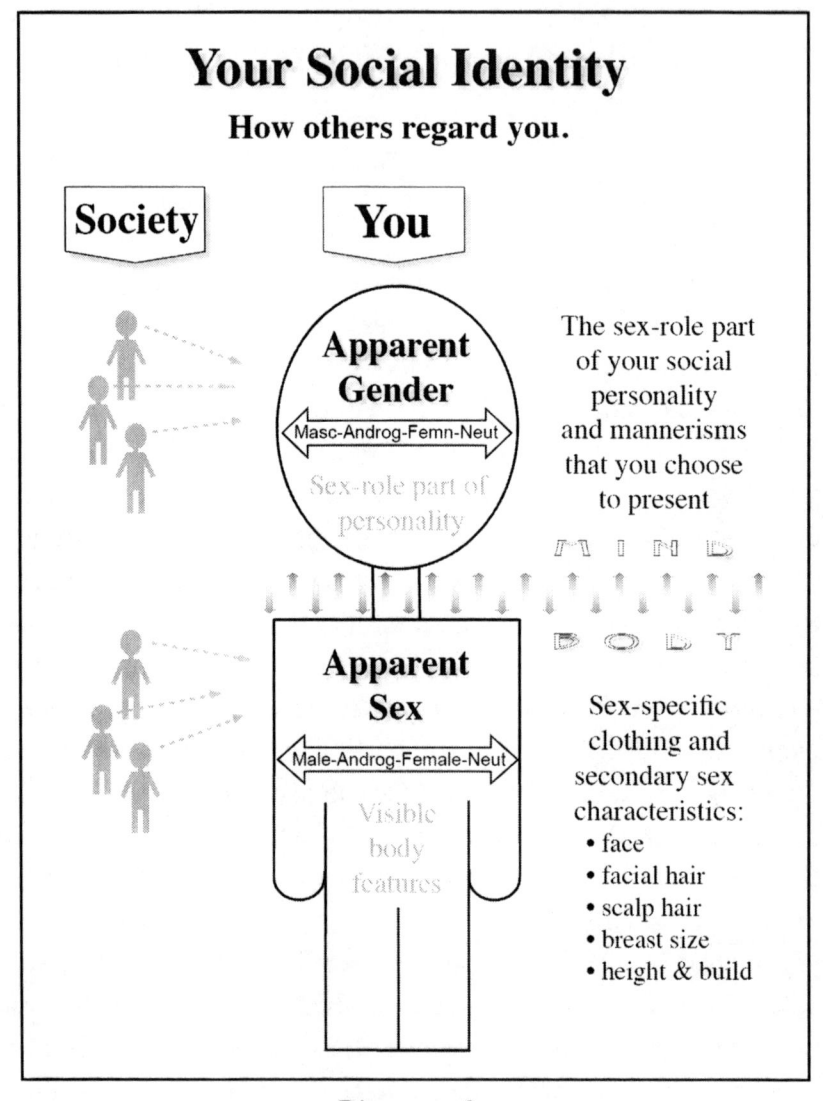

MIND

BODY

**Apparent Sex**
⟨Male-Androg-Female-Neut⟩
Visible body features

Sex-specific clothing and secondary sex characteristics:
- face
- facial hair
- scalp hair
- breast size
- height & build

Diagram 3

and lower sections labeled *Mind* and *Body*. This *loosely* divides Social Identity into Apparent Gender and Apparent Sex, respectively. The relationship between the human mind and body is complex, rather mysterious, and very individual. These arrows indicate how the body influences the mind and vice versa, and how *both* separately influence how you are regarded by others.

**Apparent Gender** is the *part* of your social personality that is influenced by your sex: it's how you *behave* publicly. It is your individual combination of gender mannerisms, presentation styles, and interests: basically the individual mix of so-called masculine and feminine traits that add up to your unique *behavioral* sexuality. Because of the pressure to fit into your binary sex-role, in reality your Apparent Gender is usually highly influenced by your Apparent Sex and all the social expectations and requirements that go with it.

Regardless of the historical social view, Apparent Gender is in fact ***not*** binary (strictly either/or), but rather a *spectrum* of *combinations* of so-called masculine and feminine traits. The double-ended arrow containing "Masculine/Androgynous/Feminine/Neuter" represents this spectrum of mixes. The fact is that most of us possess *both* masculine and feminine qualities: again these are really those *human* traits that have been artificially (and often unrealistically) assigned exclusively to males and females.

I should mention here that there exists a bit of general confusion regarding the meaning of the word "androgynous" as opposed to "neuter." Androgynous means a *combination* of *both* male/masculine and female/feminine attributes (andro meaning male, gyne female), sometimes to the point of extreme social contradiction—such as a bearded male in makeup and gown. Conversely those people who are *lacking* any clues as to whether they are male/masculine or female/feminine (due to the *absence* of telltale sex/gender markers) are essentially sex/gender *neutral* (neuter), even though some people might refer to this ambiguity as androgynous. Now you know.

It is important to recognize that gender is not only an artificial concept, its attributes vary considerably among cultures and locales. To demonstrate the inconsistency of gender expectations, simply look up the definition of the word "humane," which reads as follows:

> **humane,** *adj.* 1. having what are considered the best qualities of human beings: kind, tender, merciful, sympathetic,

etc; 2. without inflicting any more pain than is necessary; 3. with an emphasis on respect for other people's views.

The Western traditional binary sex-role view qualifies these most treasured human qualities firmly in the *feminine* gender: the class that our patriarchal society has consistently *devalued* for centuries. This cultural contradiction is but one example of the fact that human traits should not be tied strictly to one's sex.

**Apparent Sex** is perceived publicly almost entirely through our *secondary sex characteristics*. These are everything sexual *but* our genitalia: our facial features and hair, breast size, scalp hair length and style, body height and proportions, voice pitch and melody, and to a certain extent our sex-specific clothing and adornment. Our *primary* sex characteristics are our genitalia, which are seldom revealed publicly without the high risk of our subsequent incarceration.

Our Social Identity is *vastly* influenced and often strictly determined by our Apparent Sex at birth. ***The very first thing people ask about us from birth is whether we are a boy or a girl.*** This *apparent* conclusion will influence the course of our lives through very powerful and widespread social expectations.

The word "apparent" is used very carefully when referring to our sex at birth. The fact is that our visible genitalia are not the sole factor in determining our actual sex. Nor is anatomical sex as binary as society would like us to believe: that there is only male or female (see *Intersex* below).

And if we really stop to take notice of a population of individuals, *Apparent Sex* is not actually binary either. This is represented in the diagram by the double-ended arrow containing the spectrum of Male/ Androgynous/Female/Neuter. People can appear strongly male, strongly female, a combination of both (androgyny, an example of which is a masculinized female as portrayed by Demi Moore in the movie *G.I. Jane*), or appearing sexually neutral with no clues as to the anatomical sex of that individual (*who is, of course, named "Pat"*). Others of us can possess *neither* male nor female genitalia, making us "neuter;" in ancient times neutered males were referred to as "eunuchs" (transgender people *have* been around a while).

**Intersex.** It's very important to realize that the criteria for "male" and "female" classification—on which our social sex structure us built—is something that we humans have *created,* and to which nature does *not* strictly adhere. There is no better proof of this than the fact that there is significant natural occurrence of **intersex** people: those of us born with physical sex characteristics that just don't fit the definitive criteria of male or female—externally, internally, or both.

The Intersex Society of North America (ISNA) defines intersex as "*a very general term that is applied to a variety of conditions in which a person is born with a reproductive or sexual anatomy that doesn't seem to fit the typical definitions of female or male.*" The word "typical" is critical here in that "male" and "female" human anatomies are not at all consistent in nature: there is tremendous physical variation from individual to individual in both primary and secondary sex characteristics, even between "typical" males and females. ***The truth is that nature produces a spectrum of sex manifestations that stray significantly and frequently from "typical."*** The fact that our genitalia are so socially hidden from observation makes us unaware of these variations. Conversely everyone knows that noses vary in size and shape dramatically: how would one draw a sharp line between a male and female nose?

With such broad spectrums of size, shape and function, where does one decide to draw any line, beyond which an individual is not "clearly" male or female? Who decides when a penis is too small to qualify as male, or a clitoris too large for a female? These are in fact *subjective* decisions made by certain individuals who to a certain extent can't even agree amongst themselves on the delineations.

According to the ISNA there are at least 15 conditions that can qualify as intersex, involving chromosome variations, hormone insensitivities that interfere with glandular development, testicular and ovarian anomalies, the presence of both ovarian and testicular tissues, and other chemical or developmental variations from that elusive category of "typical." Intersex conditions that are actually discovered amount to an estimated 1% of all births.

The fact that we consistently refuse to accept these natural variations and integrate them into society with respect is a real tragedy: especially when you realize the ways in which these arbitrary decisions are imposed on babies who become the victims of "corrective" genital mutilations based solely on initial observation and subjective evaluation. Sexual diversity needs to be recognized as a natural phenomenon, and these children given their fundamental right to decide for themselves—at a time of *their* choosing—whether they consider themselves to be male, female, or simply an individual human being not strictly defined by either.

So once again nature proves to be non-binary; it is humans who strive to oversimplify things with artificial binary classifications.

As mentioned earlier, your Social Identity is often a compromise, limited and shaped by what is socially expected of your sex-role that's based on your Apparent Sex. But if you were somehow able to magically strip away a lifetime of social conditioning, you would find that there is a deep sense of self that lies underneath it all. It is the self-identity that lies at your core.

*(This is about the point in the TV movie you might be missing where you would be taking your first serious commercial break. Congratulations for plowing through the book this far: grab yourself some refreshments and hurry on back to this gripping thriller.)*

## On the Inside: Core Identity.

**How we really see ourselves inside.** Long before we are old enough to reason things out consciously, we as infants observe and absorb the world around us (*whilst drooling on ourselves*). We react positively or negatively to different experiences and people. And we learn quickly how our own behavior (*like drooling*) affects other people and our ability to get the things we want from day to day.

In so doing we begin to assemble a fundamental set of behaviors, likes and dislikes that form a lasting set of personal core values. This is the early formation of a **Core Identity**, the very deep sense of self that guides one's future personality development.

We'll call the *mental* and *physical* aspects of the Core Identity that are influenced by our sex our ***Gender Identity***[9] and ***Sexual Identity***[10], respectively. These two identities are distinct but not completely separate, like the two sides of a coin. It's important to realize that the relative strengths and relationship between these two elements of one's Core Identity vary from person to person. They do influence one another, so it can be hard to distinguish between them, but they operate somewhat independently on your self-awareness when you think about it.

Diagram 4 gives a visual representation of your Core Identity, and how your *mind* influences the Gender aspect of it and your *body* influences the Sexual aspect. This pair of identities represents the *part* of our total core identity that is influenced by our sexual sense of self, as is pointed out by the text below each of the spectral arrows. Our complete self-identity includes elements beyond our sexuality, such as being mammals, primates and human (*for the most part*).

## Your Core Identity
### How you regard yourself.

**You**

- **Gender Identity** — ‹Masc-Androg-Femn-Neut›
  Inner personality: part affected by sexual ID

- **Sexual Identity** — ‹Male-Intrsx-Female-Neut›
  Your inner sense of sexual self

MIND
BODY

**Reflection**

- The part of your inner personality influenced by your sexual identity

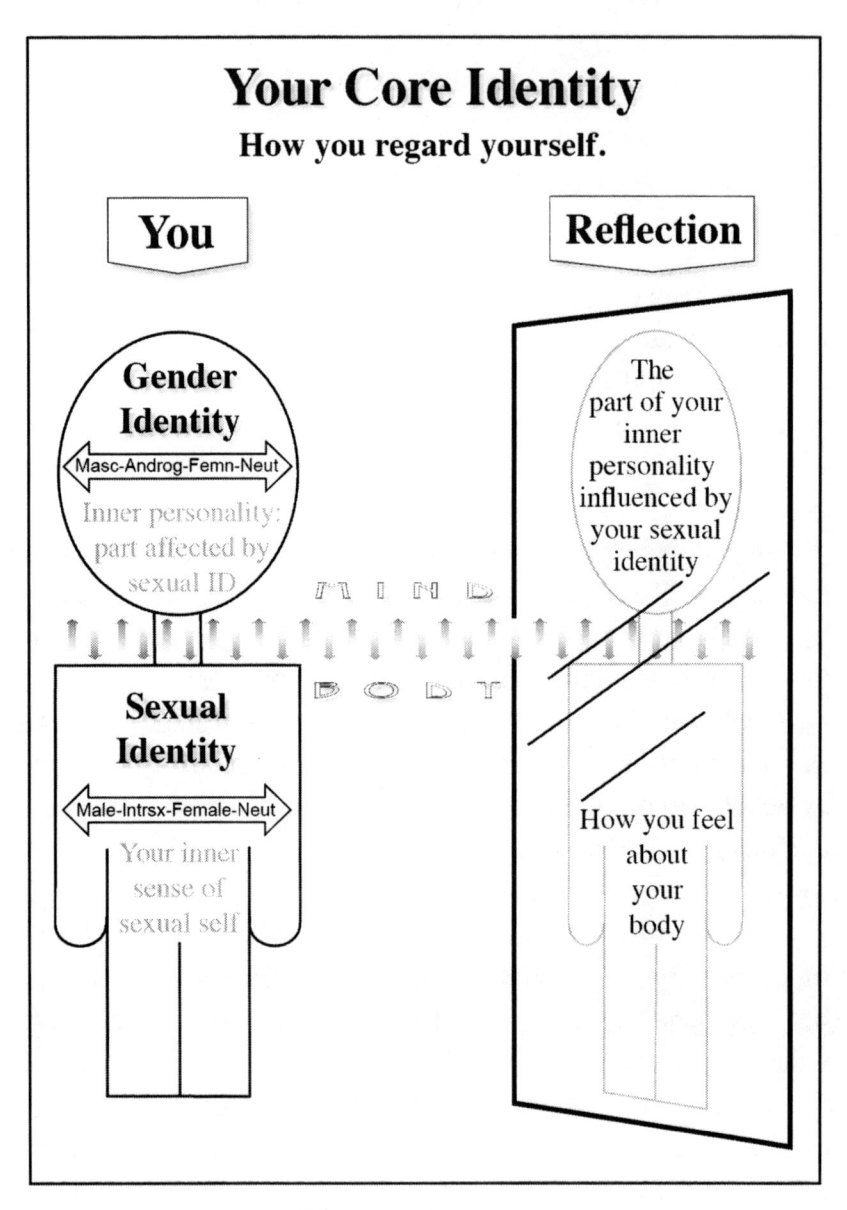

- How you feel about your body

**Diagram 4**

**Core Gender Identity** is the portion of your inner self-identity that is influenced by your sexuality. It's the *mental* sense of self that exists underneath all the social conditioning and restrictions around you, starting with its early formation in infancy as described earlier. It can be *very* difficult to painstakingly strip away a lifetime of "brainwashing" to actually determine your real values, your innermost personality. We've been told what to do, what to believe, and what to value for so long that we often end up assuming it all without question any more.

We believe it, that is, until perhaps something finally buckles and we awaken to the fact that we're NOT happy like we're supposed to be. It's often called a "mid-life crisis" (though it can happen at any time in life), and if you're transgender it is a crisis of cosmic proportions. But I digress.

Gender Identity is not binary: it's not an either/or thing. In fact most *all* humans possess a unique combination of BOTH masculine and feminine traits. Your particular Core Gender Identity falls somewhere along the *spectrum* of gender mixes (represented by the abbreviated Masculine/Androgynous/Feminine/Neuter arrow), reflecting *your* personal mix of sexually-influenced personality traits.

**Core Sexual Identity** is how we relate to our own bodies, more specifically our *physically sexual* sense of self. As mentioned earlier, our anatomical sex characteristics are divided into two classes: primary and secondary. Your sexual sense of self isn't confined to how you feel about your *genitalia*; some people feel fine about their primary sex characteristics and yet find they are uncomfortable with certain secondary sex characteristics, sex-specific body styles, clothing or adornments of their assigned birth sex. This is why certain transgender people seek to change their secondary sex-role presentation yet have no desire for genital surgery. We'll cover some specific examples of this in Part II.

Sexual Identity, like all other identities we'll talk about, is not binary: various individuals can *identify* as strongly male, strongly female, somewhere in between or neither (as represented by the Male/Intersex/Female/Neuter two-way arrow).

Many people accept their physical identity without problem, never questioning it. This is because their Core Sexual Identity happens to be more typically aligned with their assigned birth sex. This alignment occurs in a large percentage of the population, but as we now know nowhere near all of it (as proven by an emerging transgender population). A significant number of people *feel very much at odds with their genital physiology*, often from a very early age. These people are *transsexual* (a subset of transgender): they identify physiologically with a sex other than the one assigned to them at birth (see The Diversity of Transgender Identities in Part II of this book for more detail on transsexuals).

Regardless of the *actual* anatomy of your body, how you *feel* about your sexual characteristics is your Core Sexual Identity. Thus your physical sense of self can fall anywhere on the Male/Intersex/Female/Neuter spectrum.

To make sure that we avoid referring to those people who *do* more or less naturally fit into either established binary sex-role by such biased terms as "normal" or "regular" or even "straight," there are a couple of specific terms that have recently been defined.

**Cisgender and cissexual.** Biologist and author Julia Serano has proposed these two terms to describe those people whose Core Gender or Sexual Identities *do* happen to naturally *align* with their Apparent Gender or Sex, respectively.[11]

The prefix "cis-" means "subsequent to or aligned with." By combining this prefix with the word "gender," the term ***cisgender*** refers to people whose Apparent (social) Gender is *aligned with* their Core Gender Identity: they naturally fit the prevailing sex-role model of their assigned sex.

Combined with the word "sex," ***cissexual*** refers to those people whose Apparent Sex is naturally *aligned with* their Core Sexual Identity. By "naturally" I mean that these alignments exist prior to any social conditioning that pressures all of us into the binary sex-role structure.

I suspect that many of you are getting weary of trying to keep up with a plethora of "terms du jour" that are thrown at you in the name of political correctness; I would agree with that perspective myself. Yet it is very important that we take care with our language to try to take as much bias out of fundamental terms as possible. "Straight" and "normal" are highly biased terms, so we *do* need something better when talking responsibly and accurately about human sexuality.

So the terms cisgender and cissexual are important because there is a tendency in society to view social binary sex-roles as "normal" and everything else as "abnormal" and therefore "wrong" (unacceptable). This is highly inaccurate for reasons we'll discuss below. So let's talk a little more about this concept of "normal."

**Normal, average, right and wrong.** It is, in my view, sociologically dangerous to use the word "normal" instead of "average." Because doing so strongly implies that anything *not* normal is "abnormal" or "wrong." This view of "normal" probably has its roots in physiology: medically speaking we strive for health that is *normal*. Abnormality in organs and bodily functions is usually *not* good news, as we've come to assume. (*Doctor: "The scan shows that you have an abnormal spleen." Patient, blanching: "Uh-oh."*) This is because medicine takes a largely *pathological* view of not being normal (abnormalities are usually unhealthy and are therefore often deemed as pathologies).

When you get right down to it, **the concept of "normal" is just not appropriate to apply to a society of diverse individuals**. So this medical view doesn't translate well into the social sciences, where "normal" can consequently assume a strong underlying meaning of "acceptable" or "right." If you look back to even recent history, "normal" has changed a *lot* over time. Clothing that was once considered "amoral" is now pretty tame by current standards. A woman wearing a bikini publicly in 1910 would have been quickly whisked away by the local gendarmes (*to the chagrin of the overly-clad male beachcombers*).

Nonetheless, whether we're talking about mental, physical or social issues, it is not necessarily wrong *not* to be normal (average). A genius is not normal, nor is a 7' 6"-tall pro basketball player—and both are universally regarded as good things.

▽ **It is much more sociologically appropriate to use the word "average" in place of the word "normal".**

So, in order to make any discussion about gender and sex more fair and unbiased, the words cisgender and cissexual should be used since these are more specifically accurate than "normal." These terms serve an important function in taking the "deviance" stigma out of gender and sexual diversity.

**Brain sex and gender.** For ages we've assumed that *all* males "naturally" think and act one way and *all* females in an entirely different way. It's the Mars and Venus myth.[5] This is because there are certain *statistical* differences between the anatomy and—more significantly—the operation of a *typical* male brain and a *typical* female brain.[12]

The size and activity of various thought centers, as well as the neural connections between these areas, show some differences that correlate ***to a degree*** with the sexes—though these are relatively small. However, scans by functional Magnetic Resonance Imaging (fMRI) on live subjects have revealed that the way the brain is ***used*** differently by *average* males and females *can* vary more significantly, involving larger areas of the brain.[13]

Since there is a *statistical* relationship between brain physiology and sexual category, we could say that brains have an anatomical "sex": as long as we understand that like genitalia *there are more than two options.* Joan Roughgarden, Professor of Biological Sciences at Stanford University, indicates in her book *Evolution's Rainbow* that there are at least 8 different brain types based on measurable structural differences alone.[14] So let's not be hasty to assume that there are just "male" brains and "female" brains; there is a variety of structural variations in brain anatomy *and* these aren't strictly *determined* by one's sex as we might have been led to believe by our society.

Likewise we could say that the *operation* of a typical male- or female-like brain can affect its "gender" (the sex-influenced portion of personality). The fMRI scans just mentioned would be evidence of brain *gender* at work. The specific reasons why many typical males and females *use* their brains differently is still largely unknown (though it's suspected that hormones play a significant role), but this operational difference can account for some of the aptitude and behavioral trends that correlate loosely with the sexes.

It is very important to realize, though, that *many of these behavioral differences between the sexes are conditioned by culture from early childhood* because society expects and requires males and females to think only in certain ways. **The typical differences between female and male thinking are often as much artificial as they are natural.**

So to sum things up, it can be said that our *brains* have a "sex" and a "gender", BUT:

1) **Our brains are not binary**, always either strictly "male" or strictly "female" in construction or operation; instead these are *very individual* and can develop in myriad forms.

2) **The sex and/or gender of our brains does not always match the apparent sex of our bodies.** That is, males can be born with more female-type brains, and females with more male-type brains, and **this is not nearly as rare as we might think**. The emergence of a long-hidden transgender population is but one demonstration of this fact.

▼ **Each of us can have either a more statistically male-type brain or a female-type brain—or anything in between—regardless of our genitalia or chromosomal sex.**

So brain structure and operation are not strictly determined by our sex, as many cultures have assumed. This explains at least partly why there are, for example, "sensitive" males and "assertive" females: again it's a matter of *degree* that edges one into transgender territory. Outside of the realm of procreation, people are ***individuals*** first and foremost; otherwise whether one is male/intersex/female/neuter should not generally be at issue.

**The powerful role of hormones.** How powerful are they? Observe teenagers: I rest my case. Yet to understand the real *formative* power of hormones we need to go as far back as the womb (*ahh, those were the good old days*).

Scientific studies have confirmed that each fetus' response to varying levels of certain hormones at different stages of development can *independently* influence the formation of genitalia, sexual orientation, and gender identity in individuals.

In the book *Brain Sex* authors Moir and Jessel assert that variations in testosterone levels in the fetus can separately influence genital development, neural network development (thought processing), and hypothalamus development (sexual orientation) at *distinctly different times* during pregnancy.[15] After birth, spikes in hormone levels within the first year further affect gender identity, and then again shortly before puberty they influence sexual orientation.[16] ***This means that the specific "gender" of our brain and the part of it that influences our sexual orientation can develop* separately *from our genitalia and from each other.***

Both XX and XY fetuses initially possess unformed "genital duct tissue" that defaults to female without subsequent hormonal influence; and our brains all start out female (*read it and weep, boys*).[17]

The actual development of the masculine features of an XY fetus requires the aforementioned testosterone "baths" during pregnancy and further testosterone "spikes" (large short-term increases) after birth, within the first twelve months. Any variations in the levels of testosterone during these formative periods—*or* the ability of the child's body to *react* to this hormone—can produce physiological and behavioral variations from a statistical male average.

The inability of the body to *respond* to testosterone is one way in which XY babies—technically male—can develop with female features and very feminine personality to the degree that even medical personnel are convinced that the child is female (it can require internal imaging or chromosome testing to verify otherwise).

A number of case studies further indicate that *gender identity:*

a) doesn't begin to form until the beginning of the third trimester, *after* genital differentiation;

b) is well determined prior to 12 months after birth; and

c) is not reversible.[18]

I've dumped a goodly pile of bio-technicalities on you with the preceding paragraphs, but the only thing you need remember from it all is this: **these studies provide very strong biological support of the independent nature of our sexuality factors.** In other words:

▽ **There are many verifiable physiological factors that explain why gender, sexual identity and sexual orientation are not tied strictly to one's genital or chromosomal sex.**

So it is therefore biologically sound that there are indeed far more than the two forms of human sexuality that have been mandated by any binary sex-role culture.

Even after puberty, hormones play a powerful role in both behavior and physiology. This is why certain transgender people who seek to change over to their target sex undergo Hormone Replacement

Therapy (HRT). The effects of estrogen and testosterone treatments on these individuals can be quite dramatic, significantly affecting muscle mass, emotional connection, sex drive, and secondary sex characteristics such as body and scalp hair, voice pitch, breast size and body fat distribution.

**Nature or nurture: ultimately it doesn't matter.** How an individual forms a Core Identity is influenced by both *nature* and *nurture*: that is, by the physical structure of each unique brain *and* by its specific exposure to people and experiences during early infant years. There has been a lot of controversy as to whether personalities such as the transgender type are "wired in" from birth or are "chosen" through social learning and interaction.

It stands to reason, however, that *the individual structure of each unique brain can significantly influence how that individual responds to social experiences and nurturing.*[19] In other words, **nature influences nurture** (brain structure affects perception and learning). The aforementioned studies would indicate that biology plays a primary role in the early formation of a Core Identity, an identity that is permanent even though subsequent social conditioning might push it below a conscious level.

Whatever the cause behind the core identity we develop, ultimately it does not change this important ethic:

⚧ **We each have the fundamental right to embrace our true core identity and to live according to it without harm—to ourselves or anyone else.**

To suggest that our core identity is a *"lifestyle choice"* is highly inaccurate: ***we did not consciously choose much of who we fundamentally are***. A great deal of our core identity appears to develop in very early childhood, long before we acquire rational decision-making skills or even understand the concept of "lifestyle."

We can at a later point, however, choose how we *deal* with the truth of our core identity: that is the challenge that people with significantly diverse sexuality must face.

**Core identity vs. social sex-role**. You're now beginning to see that the human population actually contains a remarkable diversity of core identities that stray significantly from the social average. This guarantees that a significant percentage of the population will be pressured to live within a binary social sex-role that is wholly inappropriate for them, even intolerable. If a person's sex-role is painfully at odds with the core identity, he or she is facing the challenge of diversity (sexual or otherwise) and many tough decisions ahead.

And so, with our identities tucked under each arm (*along with the one tucked between our legs*), we go forth into the world to interact with the people around us.

## Person to Person: Relational Identity

**What attracts us to others.** Traditionally our motivation for intimate relationships has been called our *sexual orientation* (also sometimes called our sex "drive"). Whether we are attracted to the same sex, the "opposite" sex, to "both" sexes or no sex determines the social *category* of our sexual orientation: heterosexual, homosexual, bisexual or asexual.

I've placed quotes around the words "opposite" and "both" above because these existing orientation categories presume that there are only two sexes, which because of intersex variables we now know is not true (see Sexual Orientation below). Asexual means there is no *physical* attraction to any sex (*this could be considered good news or bad news, depending on your particular experience with sexual intimacy*).

As we better understand the dual mind/body nature of someone's core identity, however, it makes sense that we can have attractions to a person's *personality* aspects (including gender) that are distinct from the physiological ones. So we could say that we each have a certain **Gender Orientation** and a certain **Sexual Orientation**, and these combine to form our overall **Relational Identity:** how we identify ourselves from an attraction standpoint.

The coin analogy also works well here: our Gender and Sexual Orientations are two sides of the same coin that we call Relational Identity, shown visually in Diagram 5.

Once again the diagram shows how the Mind influences the Gender part and the Body influences the Sexual aspect of our Relational Identity. And since people's sex influences their gender these are related and sometimes tricky to separate in our minds.

The Diversity of Human Sexuality 49

## Your Relational Identity
**How you regard others.**

**You**     **Society**

**Gender Orientation**
‹Hetero-homo-bi-a-gender›
Other sex-roles that attract you

The social sex-role part of personalities that attract you.

MIND
BODY

**Sexual Orientation**
‹Hetero-homo-bi-a-sexual›
Attraction to sexual anatomy

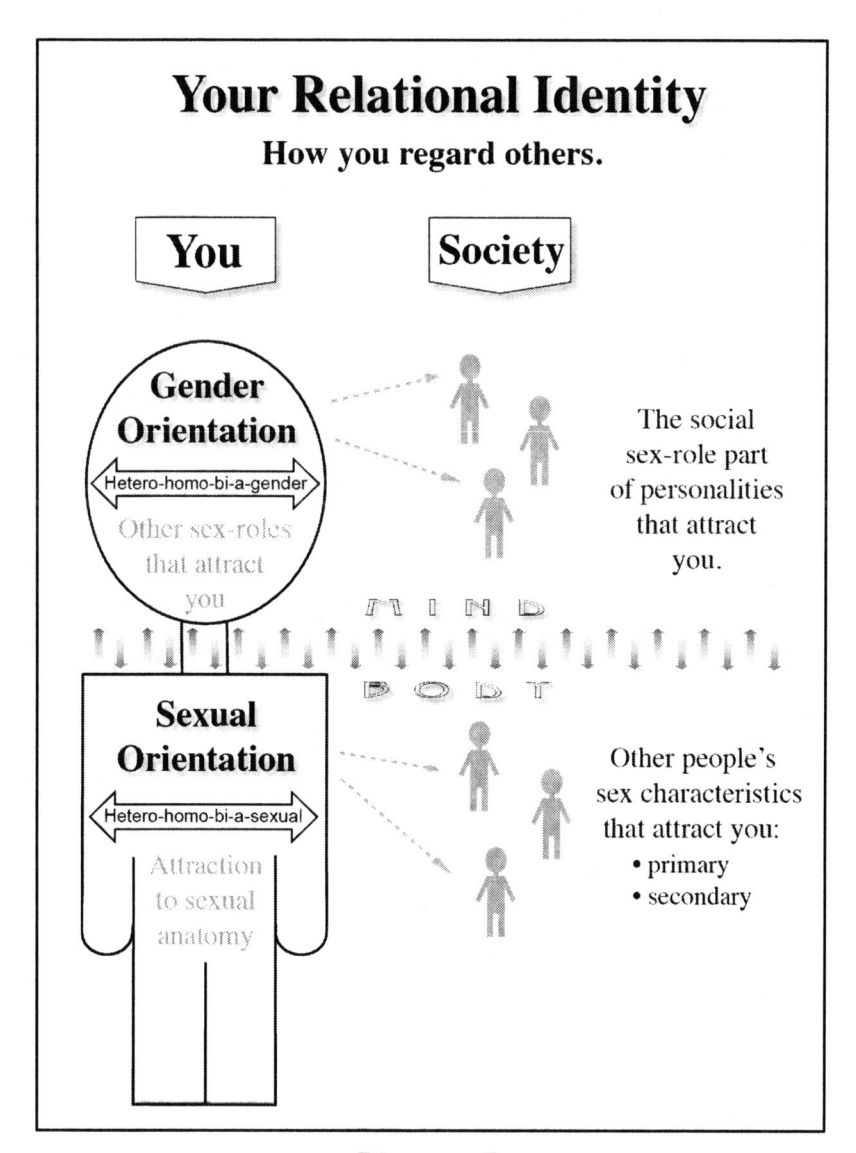

Other people's sex characteristics that attract you:
• primary
• secondary

Diagram 5

    **Gender Orientation** refers to the types of gender presentations (the sexual aspect of personality) that attract us. This orientation is truly distinct from the sexual one—even though we might have assumed that our attractions were all purely physical. Gender orientation often becomes more apparent later on in a relationship after the sex drive settles down a bit—as it usually does. We often discover that Gender Orientation can be at least as strong as, if not stronger than, the Sexual one—and more durable, as a rising divorce rate might suggest (due significantly to incompatible *personalities*, of which "gender" can be a large part).

How we feel emotionally about someone can dramatically affect our physical response to them, as most of us have experienced when intense love or infatuation greatly augments our sexual attraction. Furthermore relational conflicts or outside stress, which are most often mental, can completely remove physical attraction and sexual response to the partner (*embarrassingly obvious for males*), even though physical attributes haven't changed at all. Some cultures even base relational orientation solely on gender rather than sex.[20]

Say you are attracted to the anatomy of a male. Would you be happier in the long run with a more masculine male or a more feminine one? Or do you want both at different times? This is Gender Orientation at work. The Hetero-homo-bi-a-gender double-ended arrow in the diagram visually represents the spectrum of gender preferences we can have.

**Sexual Orientation** you surely know about. It refers to the sexual *anatomies* that attract us. Sexual Orientation is not binary (either/or) but rather a spectrum of possibilities, as represented by the double-ended Hetero-homo-bi-pan-a-sexual arrow ("pansexual" is explained in the next paragraph). For example, someone can be bisexual but slightly prefers males to females.

This is a good time to open your mind a little to the concept of sexual orientation in a population of diverse sexualities; that is, more than two sexes and sex-roles. The natural existence of intersex people, as well as the myriad forms of sexual identities, makes it appropriate to use the term "pansexual" in addition to "bisexual." Pansexual people are by definition physically attracted to many forms of physiology (more than just two, as "bisexual" indicates). This is a relatively new term that is increasingly popular in the gender queer population (see *The Diversity of Transgender Identities* in Part II of this book).

Another term related to bisexual and pansexual is *polyamorous*. This generally refers to having more than one intimate relationship concurrently, and can often involve various sex and gender presentations.

There are many people who might find these iterations of sexual intimacy morally offensive. But I would remind you that as long as no rights are violated and you are not forced to be involved, we *all* have the civil right to live according to our personal beliefs—as long as no one is harmed. It's not the purpose of this book to advocate for or against the many relational forms mentioned herein, but rather to expose you to the actual diversity that is expressed in the real world.

Sometimes the term "sexual preference" is used instead of "sexual orientation;" but the word "preference" denotes a conscious choice as opposed to the early orientation development that precedes rational skills—as described earlier in *The powerful role of hormones*. The overwhelming majority of LGBT people confirm that their orientation was not a conscious choice, so I will use the more appropriate term "orientation" in this book. (See *Sexual preference* in the Glossary at the end of this book.)

**A further word on asexual orientation.** A good way to understand asexual orientation is that some folks are exclusively attracted to people's individual personality and values—including gender—and not at all to their sexual characteristics. This sheds a more appropriate light on the fact that asexual people are *not* devoid of attraction or feelings for others, as the term "asexual" might be erroneously interpreted. Rather the richness and depth of their feelings are focused on *mind* (or *soul*: many believe that souls have no sex) rather than body—which is a perfectly valid place to be in our sexuality model.

**When categories become counterproductive.** There comes a point where the creation of artificial classes begins to do more harm than good. With every new category, individuality is put more at risk. So in dealing with such highly individual animals as humans there'd better be a darn good reason for every category we manage to dream up.

It's the old cart-before-the-horse thing. As we discussed previously, there is high danger that categories begin to define people within them instead of vice versa. With every action we take in day-to-day life, we're susceptible to being classified by it in some way, thereby opening up the opportunity for discrimination and prejudice of all kinds. And one classification we simply can't escape is that of the "type" of sexual orientation we profess—with considerable social pressure to claim the proper one.

As studies such as the Kinsey Reports[3] revealed, many people will confide to having an inner sexual orientation that is not the one they show publicly because of the powerful social pressure against it. Others are conditioned so thoroughly by parents and society that they are fearful to admit *even to themselves* any relational orientation that is not publicly acceptable, real though it may be.

When folks finally proclaim an inner sexual orientation that's been hidden, they can appear to "make a choice" to "change" their sexual "preferences." The same goes for transgender people who might seem to change their sexual orientation after they transition to another sex-role. On the contrary these are virtually always the public revelation of a core identity that's been there from the beginning.

▽ **People who appear to change sexual orientation later in life are most often addressing a core identity that has *been there all along*, though deeply suppressed through social conditioning.**

On the other hand, some transgender people may retain their orientation type even after recognizing and professing an inner core identity. For example, if a person assigned male self-identifies as heterosexual—attracted to females—this person *may* remain heterosexual after transition—now attracted to males—because the inner desire for a relationship with "otherness" responds to the recognized female core identity. Other TG's born male and heterosexual may retain their attraction to females, thus their orientation class "changes" from hetereo- to homosexual. It's all valid (*albeit a bit puzzling at times*).

So the point in all this is that relational identity and core identity are not necessarily bound together, that each transgender individual's relational identity may respond uniquely to the discovery of an inner core identity. As mentioned earlier, core gender and relational identities involve distinctly different areas of the brain.

**The myth of the "lifestyle choice."** There is a widespread popular belief that having a diverse sexual orientation is a "lifestyle choice." Those of us who honestly experience sexual and/or gender diversity couldn't disagree more.

As mentioned earlier in the *Nature vs. nurture* section, these identities and orientations are pretty much wired in from a period before and shortly after birth, as the ongoing progress of medical, psychiatric and psychological research bears out.[21]

If you are one that shares the lifestyle choice view, I would ask that you *suspend* this view at least momentarily and *consider* some of the perspectives that are offered herein: you still have the choice to retain your opinion in the end. Be open-minded while you read this short book (*nobody's watching*).

# The Whole Picture

So the model I'm offering in this book proposes that our individual sexuality is comprised of our own unique combination of the three mind/body pairs of variables: our Social Identities, Core Identities, and Relational Identities. The relative strengths and relationships of these factors seem to strongly influence how we think about ourselves, how we present ourselves to society, and how we relate to others socially and intimately.

**The six variables of sexuality.** As you can see by Diagram 6 there is *tremendous* potential for diversity by the time you factor in the six separate ***spectrums*** of Gender Identity, Sexual Identity, Apparent Gender, Apparent Sex, Gender Orientation and Sexual Orientation. Each of these factors has virtually infinite possibilities, so the range of combined variables is *staggering*. No *wonder* there is an emerging population of gender and sexual diversity!

So: hopefully *now* you have a better idea why so many people feel (even if they don't admit it to anyone out loud or even to themselves) that they don't fit into an overly simplistic and restrictive binary sex-role system that many societies have mandated for centuries.

And remember: **this diagram applies to *every* human being**, not just diverse people. Take some time and see how it applies to YOU—it will be a fascinating process I assure you.

**If there is one thing that you take away from this book,** I hope it's a clearer understanding of the fundamental *complexity* of human sexuality; that it is inevitable that the natural diversity of gender and sexual identities eventually break free from a constrictive binary

# The Diversity of Human Sexuality

## How others regard you.
### Social Identity

**Apparent Gender**
⟨Masc-Androg-Femn-Neut⟩
The sex-role part of your social personality

**Apparent Sex**
⟨Male-Androg-Female-Neut⟩
Sex-typed clothing and secondary sex characteristics
• face • facial hair
• scalp hair • breast size • body height & build • etc.

## How you regard yourself.
### Core Identity

**Gender Identity**
⟨Masc-Androg-Femn-Neut⟩
Inner personality: part affected by sexual ID

**Sexual Identity**
⟨Male-Intrsx-Female-Neut⟩
Your inner sense of sexual self

## How you regard others.
### Relational Identity

**Gender Orientation**
⟨Hetero-homo-bi-a-gender⟩
Other sex-roles that attract you

**Sexual Orientation**
⟨Hetero-homo-bi-a-sexual⟩
Other people's sex characteristics that attract you:
• primary (genitalia)
• secondary

## Diagram of Human Sexuality Variables

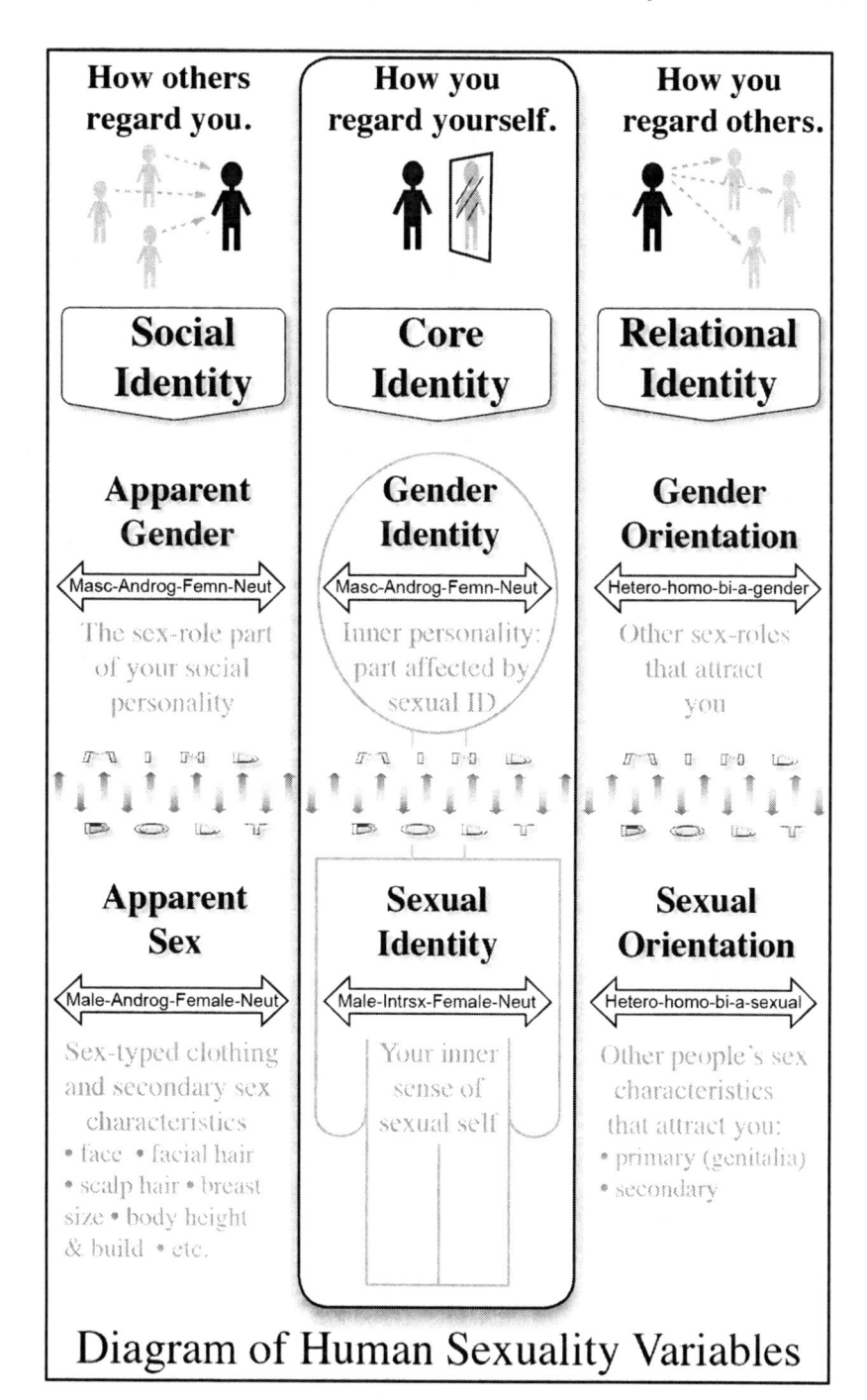

Diagram 6

sex-role system: thanks in large part to the Information Age.

It should make a lot more sense to you (*enlightened as you now are*) that a significant number of people are now discovering that in spite of following society's sex-role instructions, things just aren't working out. They keep on having "these feelings that won't stop haunting me, no matter how hard I try to avoid them." And eventually they consider confronting these feelings, instead of running from them. And through education they find that these feelings may in fact not be a *disorder*, but rather a perfectly natural human experience.

The next step, then, is to figure out exactly what is going on, why the angst and confusion and depression just won't go away. Hopefully we eventually find out that no search for fulfillment can be successful before looking in the most critical direction: *inward*.

# The Diversity of Human Sexuality

# II.

# The Spectrum of Transgender Expression

## Transgender Self-discovery

As we discussed earlier, people identify as transgender when their core identities conflict significantly with their social identities (their required social sex-roles). The strength of early social conditioning usually overpowers most transgender children's efforts to express their core identity: it doesn't fit into the binary system, and by golly it is *not* tolerated. In fact, a child's core identity can be shoved so deeply below the conscious mind that it can take decades, if ever, to re-discover it.

**Feelings: pathways around conditioning**. Since childhood sex-role conditioning is applied *over* a TG's permanent core identity, it takes constant positive/negative reinforcement and even punishment—from parents, loved ones, relatives, friends, co-workers, the media, *everyone*—to keep an inner sense of self and values suppressed. But there *is* a route from the core subconscious self up and around the conditioned mind: *feelings*.

When transgender people witness visual cues or behaviors around them that resonate with their hidden core identity, they get these *feelings*. Some young girls want to dress and act like boys because it feels so *right*. Some young boys secretly wear their sister's or Mom's clothing or underwear because it *feels* deeply wonderful. They do so even though they rationally know that they're not *supposed* to feel good doing these things.

But there is a price for breaking social rules: *guilt*. That's a feeling, too, and it goes to war with those deeper feelings trying to break through, trying to release a core identity. This tug-of-war can go on for years, resulting in a cycle of giving in to deeper feelings, followed by guilt and then denial.

This is a cycle that most cross-dressers are all too familiar with—and most TGs cross-dress at some time in their lives (though females have more leeway in presentation, so "cross"-dressing can be less apparent). Clothing is secretly acquired, hidden, and donned in nerve-wracking privacy. Then comes the guilt, the denial, the purging of clothing, and another attempt to bury the feelings.

(*Directions for cross-dressing: obtain other-sex clothing; apply liberally. Side effects include severe guilt. Dispose after use. Repeat until something snaps. See your doctor.*)

▼ **Feelings are important clues that something is going on deep inside, something we need to listen to and be allowed to explore.**

There is a saying among transgender people that "*you can't outrun this thing.*" Eventually, one way or another, the core identity breaks through for an increasing number of TGs. Then the challenges accelerate.

**A compass to your core.** True happiness is, after all, a *feeling*. In the end, only *you* can know what brings you true joy and fulfillment. It is the *true* part that is challenging. In other words:

▼ **Only those things that resonate with our core values will actually elicit a feeling of true happiness.**

Which is why connecting with your own core identity is so critical to your happiness; false identities can only experience incomplete happiness. *This applies to everyone, not just transgender people.*

The tough part about finding core values is the meticulous stripping away of a mountain of instructions we were *told* we needed to follow in order to be happy or accepted. It takes real honesty to stop and ask, "How do I, myself, *really* feel about this?"

⚧ **The binary sex-role perspective permeates virtually every aspect of our thinking, which can make it very difficult to access any core values that have been buried by a lifetime of social conditioning.**

Identifying our real values means re-assessing everything, including sensitive sexuality issues, with absolute honesty and without guilt. Yes, much easier said than done. Many transgender people have associated guilt and rejection with their inner feelings for so long that it can be *very* difficult to consider that these feelings might actually *not* be wrong.

Feelings are compasses that can help guide anyone, including a transgender person, to their core identity and values. The source for each feeling will hopefully come to light eventually, but it is the feeling that points us in a particular direction. It ultimately may not turn out to be a *good* direction (i.e. harmful to yourself or others), but you'll only find out by examining these rather than suppressing them. Notice I said *examine*, not "give in to."

Most mental health professionals will tell you that feelings are in and of themselves neither good nor bad. *It is how we **respond** to these feelings that can be constructive or destructive*—to ourselves and/or other people. Those who respond destructively to feelings shouldn't be allowed to do so *if*—and only if—it *actually* and objectively threatens their well-being or that of anyone around them.

That being said, we must be careful about interpreting the concept of "threaten." For example, sexual diversity may "threaten" my beliefs by being "morally offensive," but *if no one is forcing this diversity on anyone then I have no civil right to prevent others from holding and practicing (at least privately) their beliefs.*

It's the "live and let live" principle, a simple but seemingly impossible "golden rule" to achieve by our species. Our ability to tolerate different but non-interfering religious, social and political practices has been tragically and fatally lacking over the millennia. (We'll go into this in greater depth at the end of Part III.)

# The Spectrum of Transgender Expression

**Eureka! . . . *now* what?** If TGs *finally* (with luck) experience the epiphany of re-discovering and embracing their core identity, and then find it to be in extreme conflict with their prescribed sex-role, they now stand at the brink of a truly daunting life dilemma. This is because two very fundamental needs are painfully at odds with one another.

**To be or to belong.** Somewhat reminiscent of Shakespeare's famous line, this phrase not only describes the pair of basic needs we all have, but the frequent experience of having these needs pulling in opposing directions if we're a little "different" from the rest of the crowd. Simply put:

▽ **As self-conscious and social beings, we are saddled with two fundamental needs: the need to be ourselves and the need to belong.**

Sometimes these needs are aligned: you can be yourself and naturally fit in with friends and/or society. But often they are in significant opposition: you must be like *them* to fit in, even though it is not really *you* at all. This fact contributes to the angst of many teenagers who are dealing with so many aspects of identity and relationships, with so little experience from which to draw.

Actress Felicity Huffman, in speaking of her academy award nomination for her role in the movie *Trans America* as a trans woman, described the transgender dilemma very well:

*"Transgender people are faced with an untenable choice, which is: if they decide NOT to go through with the transformation, then they are alienated from their true selves. If they decide TO go through with it then they are alienated from society."*

This is the dilemma that most self-identified transgender people face. It is a most difficult situation, one that taxes many TGs to their limits and all too often beyond.

Perhaps the strongest message of the transgender experience is that ***the need to be one's true self is often more critical than the need to belong***. When you think about it, if you are not yourself then you can't fully experience what life has to offer; few of us would choose to live a hollow existence. An increasing number of transgender individuals are affirming the validity of this perspective by literally risking *everything* (family ties, careers, a place to live and more) to openly become their true selves—sometimes to the point of suffering terrible hate crimes.

**A hierarchy of human needs**. We spend the bulk of our lives striving to survive myriad challenges and, if we're lucky, to prosper. Most of us would agree that there is a general priority to our needs in life: water, food, shelter, companionship, esteem and so on.

Psychologist Abraham Maslow developed an interesting model to graphically display these priorities.[22] One version is displayed as a

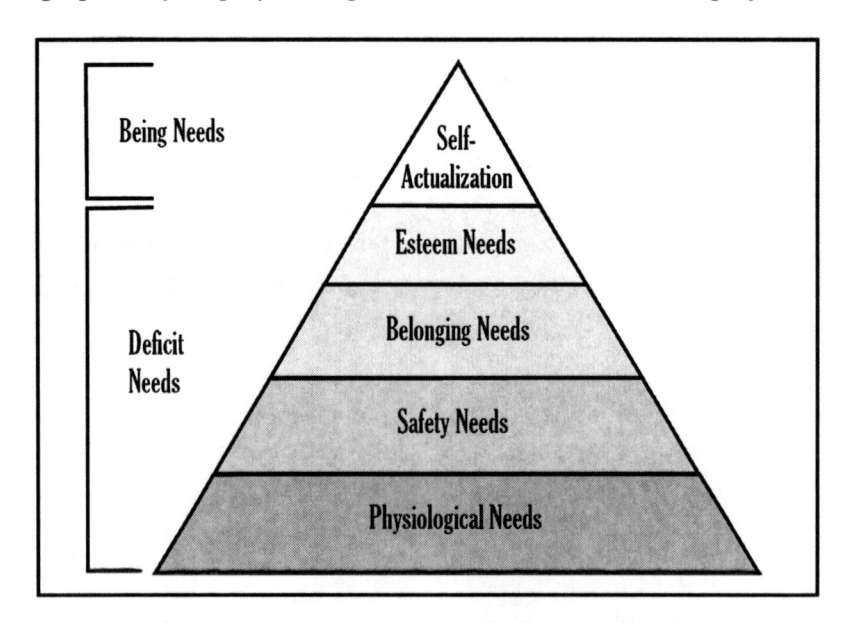

Diagram 7: Maslow's Hierarchy of Needs

pyramid, as shown in Diagram 7. There has been some psychological controversy as to whether any hierarchy of human needs—if such even exists—is as consistent or well-defined as that proposed by Maslow. Even so, generally speaking we *tend* to prioritize basic physical survival needs over the more intellectual ones, so Maslow's pyramid is a useful graphic presentation by which we can begin to grasp how high the priority of identity expression is for transgender people.

**Coming out as transgender = back to square one**. When a TG finally decides to make his or her truth known, almost every other need in life is now at risk. So in a sense a TG's pyramid is turned topside down with the decision for self-actualization. This is portrayed by the appropriately modified pyramid in Diagram 8.

Apparently none of the Egyptian Pharaohs was transgender, to the vast relief of their engineers. Humor definitely aside (though TGs have chuckled knowingly at this quip in my classes), you could

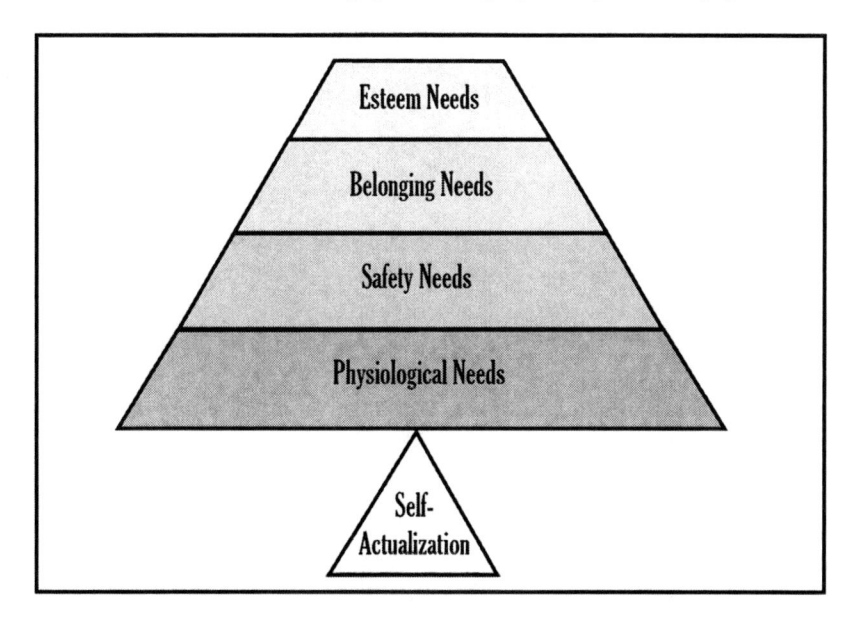

Diagram 8: A Transgender Hierarchy of Needs

put it this way:

▽ **Everything in a transgender person's life literally hangs in the balance at the point of self-actualization: when his or her truth is revealed publicly.**

For such a TG, the need to be true to one's self is most powerful indeed: so strong that *all other aspects of that person's life are poised to topple into loss*. When TGs announce their transgender nature, their jobs, relationships, even places to live can be put in serious jeopardy. This gives us a pretty good idea of how fundamentally critical it is to these people that they live openly as their real selves. For some transgender folks it is literally a matter of survival.

# Responding to the Core

Once a transgender person does, by hook or crook, discover and/or embrace a true core identity, each individual must decide how specifically to respond to this truth. Realizing that one is transgender is usually mixed news at best. I happened to stumble upon a daytime talk show in the mid-1980s that hosted three local cross-dressers when it finally hit me—the proverbial ton of bricks—what had really been going on inside me all these years. My reaction was equal parts joy and dread: I didn't know whether to jump up and click my heels or assume the fetal position and tremble.

**Making adjustments.** Responding to a clarified core identity often precipitates some kind of adjustment to a TG's life. Whether it is minor or major depends on the current state of affairs and where he or she wants to go from this point onward.

Sometimes the risk for significant change, or even the slightest revelation of this deep secret, is too great to pursue: it's just not worth it for many TGs. That's a decision—hopefully based on objective consideration rather than fear alone—that each person must make individually.

Quite often, though, the clarification of a long suppressed core identity is *very* strong motivation to enable this truth to be made manifest, incorporated somehow into this TG's life. I'll describe some of the general ways that people can respond to these identities in the next section on transgender diversity.

After a lifetime of suppression, it is difficult enough for a TG to uncover a long-buried core identity. Once everything finally "makes sense now," the yearning to immediately pursue and express one's true self often becomes unbearable (i.e. "damn the torpedoes, full speed ahead"). But the urge to sprint into action is quickly dampened by a very thick social brick wall looming dead ahead on the road to self-actualization.

**Society's response: it doesn't fit, therefore it's not allowed.** When the stress of a repressed core identity reaches critical mass at some point in a TG's life, the truth must come out and confrontation with society begins—usually with the immediate family. Unfortunately, society's reaction has been historically very strong and very negative. And you now know why:

▽ **Gender variance doesn't fit into the narrow confines of a binary sex-role social structure, and is therefore not well tolerated.**

We have been expected for centuries to live within either of only two very restrictive sex-roles, for sociopolitical and religious reasons too innumerable get into here. The bottom line is that gender variance has historically been viewed as "abnormal" or "deviant" and therefore unacceptable behavior. This is in fact oppressive for *both* males and females, not to mention intersex folks, requiring many people to be much less than their whole selves. It begs the question *who*, then, defines "normal" in our society?

**Who decides what is "normal"?** We need to understand that the concept of "normal" (that we touched on earlier) is not completely created and maintained by professionals. It is the *prevailing social view of "normal" that most strongly influences its definition in any locale or period in time*. Psychiatrists and psychologists often adjust diagnoses and thinking *in response to social mores*, to become consistent with the majority. In other words:

▽ **The definition of "normal" is heavily influenced by the prevailing** social viewpoint, not science alone.

A good example of this is the response of the ongoing editions of the Diagnostic Statistical Manual of psychiatry (called the DSM) to the social struggle with sexual orientation (chiefly homosexuality). It took a significant segment of the population to declare their non-heterosexual nature, challenge social discrimination, and precipitate the necessary sociopolitical awareness to affect scientific change. The psychiatric diagnosis of homosexuality as a *disorder* was then removed from the DSM-II, the second revised edition of the Diagnostic Statistical Manual (the actual process, beginning in 1973, is a bit complicated but eventually this disorder was removed altogether from the DSM by 1986).

**Whose disorder is it, anyway?** The current psychiatric diagnostic manual, the **DSM-IV-TR**, describes a certain **condition** (not a *disorder*) called **gender dysphoria**, in which a person exhibits *"persistent discomfort with his or her sex or sense of inappropriateness in the gender role of that sex."*[23] In other words, it's the unhappiness a person feels because his or her core identity doesn't match the sex and/or sex-role assigned at birth.

If a person's gender dysphoria escalates to the degree that it *"causes clinically significant distress or impairment in social, occupational, or other important areas of functioning,"* he or she can be diagnosed with **Gender Identity Disorder**, which is #302-6 in the DSM IV-TR.[23] It is abbreviated **GID**. A disorder is basically a diagnosed form of mental impairment or dysfunction.

▼ **It is important to understand that it is society's refusal to tolerate gender diversity that can precipitate gender dysphoria and GID. Gender variance is not, in and of itself, necessarily a disorder.**

Stop for a moment and *really think about this*. People diagnosed with GID are not necessarily dysfunctional in and of themselves; it is society's relentless suppression of human diversity that can often precipitate a disorder.

It is also important to understand that gender dysphoria cannot be resolved through psychological re-programming of the core identity, a fact recognized by the psychiatric community.[23] In other words,

▼ **GID can't be "cured" or erased mentally but rather *resolved* by modifying the social role and/or the body of that person to align these with the core identity.**

GID can be thought of as a disorder from the persistent deprivation of a fundamental human need. Like the "disorder" a political prisoner would experience when locked away for life. Freedom—from either the concrete prison or the sex-role prison—is quite likely to resolve such a "disorder."

Bluntly:

▼ **GID is not necessarily the transgender person's problem: it is most often *society's* problem.**

We talked about cross-dressing a bit earlier as a frequent outlet for the feelings trying to get around a TG's rational conditioning. Cross-dressing is but one form of transgender expression: there are countless more ways to respond to a transgender identity. The next section will present *some* of the well-populated forms of expression to give you an indication of the variety of transgender identities.

# The Diversity of Transgender Identities

**It's all about individuality.** Human beings are highly complicated creatures, both mentally and physiologically. The amazing extent of our organic complexity alone ensures the statistical impossibility that any two of us will be exactly alike: we are a species of individuals. In fact, there are so many variables in our biology, function and experiences that we are very likely to differ *significantly* from one individual to another.

However, this diversity of individuals complicates a very strong instinct for survival, one that drives us to create two very fundamental human categories: friend or foe. *Self-defense, in myriad forms, often lies at the root of our need to discriminate our differences.*

The fact is that for millennia humans have obsessively created all manner of categories at every opportunity, after which we set about shoving each other into them with abandon. Race, ethnicity, creed, sex, geography: you name it. And of course two major categories that many cultures have maintained throughout the centuries are the binary sex-roles of females and males: woman and man, respectively.

In addition to an animal instinct for survival, however, humans are uniquely *self-conscious* beings, each possessing the deep desire to be recognized and appreciated as an individual (the need to *be* as well as belong). In a very fundamental way, transgender emergence is but one example of an underlying pressure to move away from categories and toward the recognition of individuality.

So even though we've defined a category of humans we call "transgender," this group is entirely populated by *individuals*. Knowing how many variables there are that make up our individual sexualities, it should then be no surprise that there are countless ways to be "transgender." In fact:

⚧ **There are as many ways to be transgender as there are transgender people.**

Most people don't realize this. Even many TGs *themselves* don't understand this important truth. There is a tendency to think that there is only one pathway (a progression) to follow to be transgender, which is certainly not universally true. We'll talk about this shortly.

There is a strong and pervasive social force, conditioned into us since birth, that seeks to conform us to the established binary sex-role structure. Consequently there is an assumption that all transgender people ultimately seek *exclusively* to move completely from one stereotypical sex-role to "the" other: *to stay well within the binary* (thereby preserving the system rather than expanding it).

Societies tend to conclude that all transgender people are basically *transsexual* (eventually seeking sex-change surgery), in order to maintain the binary congruence of sex and gender. It is therefore assumed that various transgender forms such as cross-dressing or gender variance are just stages of progression along the single path to this transsexual end. Sorry, no way, ix-nay on that: just ask a large segment of the transgender population.

Binary thinking also lies at the root of the common question initially asked after a transgender announcement: "Does this mean you're gay?" Because a sex-change "corrects" what would be a homosexual condition back to the socially preferred heterosexual one.

Remember that each of the six facets of our identity is a *spectrum*, with nearly infinite possibilities. Half of these involve the body, and half involve the *mind*. Many transgender people don't desire and shouldn't undergo surgeries or even spend full time in either binary social sex-role.

Many TGs are best fulfilled by regularly moving from one role to another—or shifting around in the middle ground continuously—thus enjoying a variety of human experience that many people confined to the binary extremes may not. Hold this thought: we'll examine many of these options shortly.

**Different transgender identities are *distinct* as opposed to being stages of a singular progression**. Again, transgender people don't necessarily start at point A and then work all or part way to a singular endpoint Z: a progression. A TG can embrace any identity, go in its general direction to an *individual* destination, or even move from one identity to another as he or she grows in self-understanding.

*However*: since some of these identities involve irreversible medical treatments, extreme care must be used during the discovery process. It is *highly* recommended and usually required that professional psychological and medical consultation be utilized before ANY physiological treatments are considered. I would be remiss if I didn't point out that many TGs obtain hormones on the black market: this is very risky, as hormones can have formidable side effects (i.e. some might be good, but more can kill you).

**The inherent danger of categories**. As we just discussed, humans have long been driven to create all manner of social categories and then shove each other into them, with the effect of homogenizing and de-personalizing everyone to varying degrees. Whenever we define some category, for whatever reason, it can wind up unreasonably *defining* the people in it—and we can consequently abandon any desire to know any one of them as discrete individuals. This process of "de-humanizing" paves the way for discrimination of all kinds. It has served as a conduit through which untold suffering and death has been perpetrated for centuries.

So it is with a certain trepidation that I present the following very *general* transgender distinctions (dangerously suggestive of categories). While these brief overviews would help you get a better understanding of the diversity of the transgender experience, ***there is a terrible danger that any individual distinguished by a certain general characteristic will be summarily defined by it***, and thus the individuality for which we each strive will be instantly hamstrung.

In any case it would be helpful to describe a number of the more fundamental distinctions between many transgender individuals, to better understand how different sexuality variables are actually expressed. It's natural, after all, that folks who share a lot in common will be drawn together socially—which is what populates the groups in which these individuals place themselves. Just remember:

**▼ Ultimately we need to recognize and embrace human individuality, not categories or profiles.**

**A number of basic transgender distinctions**. If you'll remember our definition of "transgender" at the beginning of this book, it involves three ways to cross sex-role boundaries: 1) clothing and adornment, 2) personality and mannerisms, and 3) bodily features. Each of the following *general* transgender forms deals with one or more of these means of expression.

There is another factor, however, that plays an important role in distinguishing between different gender and/or sexual identities, and that is whether a transgender expression is embraced ***part-time*** or ***full-time***. When, for example, a male crossdresser decides to transition to a full-time trans woman, there can be a significant shift in the way she perceives her identity experience and how she is regarded by others. Her feminine expression shifts from an occasional special event to an everyday thing, in itself quite significant as you might imagine. These factors are worthwhile to note because they help make clear the tremendous diversity *within* the transgender population itself.

**Crossdresser:** *part-time appearance change.* One who receives fulfillment and/or pleasure by dressing in the clothes normally reserved for another sex-role; this involves a change of clothes and adornment, but not a significant change in psychological behavior (i.e. gender).

**Cogender (or Bigender):** *part-time appearance and behavior change.* Applies to those who cross-dress in order to feel free to express an inner gender identity. This allows for an ongoing balance between two relatively polarized gender roles: masculine and feminine. A significant change in personality accompanies the change of clothes. (I am proposing the term "cogender" to mean two polar genders *co*-existing in the same person; bigender better describes the gender *orientation* counterpart to bisexual, and we need to be distinct wherever possible to minimize confusion.)[24]

**Transsexual:** *full-time appearance, behavior and genital change.* Describes those who identify as a *sex* other than that assigned at birth, which is distinct from identifying as another *gender*. The desired resolution of this identity is often Genital Reassignment Surgery (GRS). The term "transsexual" is more commonly applied to male-to-female identities, to distinguish these from the part-time cross-dressers (or the obsolete term "transvestites") and drag queens for which they can sometimes be mistaken. Since there is no significant female social counterpart to crossdresser (or "transvestite") from which they need to distinguish, female-to-male TGs usually prefer the term "trans man" as opposed to transsexual (see *Trans Man and Trans Woman* below). There are three states of transsexuality: pre-op (short for pre-operative), post-op and non-op. Since transsexuals are required to live for at least a year full time in their desired social role prior to genital surgery, they spend a lot of time being pre-op. And because surgery is *very* expensive, they can spend even more time in this state saving up the funds. Then there are those who *can't* have GRS.

**Non-op transsexual:** *full-time appearance, behavior, some body change.* Although technically transsexual, most individuals who identify as another sex are (sadly) *unable* to undergo GRS for financial, health, or other reasons. This is not a choice. Hormone therapy is usually adopted to help achieve as much bodily form of the target sex as possible, health permitting.

**Trans man and trans woman:** *full-time appearance, behavior, any body change desired.* Since surgery is not the defining factor of transgender people, the terms *trans man* and *trans woman* are increasingly favored to describe a full-time sex-role change. These terms do not signify whether GRS has been undergone or not, which is more appropriate to the public identity of transgender people. Moreover, many transgender individuals *choose* to retain their birth genitalia even though they live their lives full-time in the social *role* of the target sex. Trans man means *trans*gender person now living as a *man*, and likewise trans woman means *trans*gender person now living as a *woman*. These terms are used increasingly instead of "transsexual" even for male-to-female TGs. Hormone replacement therapy and perhaps various surgeries (sometimes including GRS) are undergone to satisfy their identity and role needs.

**Queer, gender queer or gender variant:** *part- or full-time appearance, behavior, and possible body change.* A growing number of diversely identified people, especially younger folks, refuse to be squeezed into either binary sex-role extreme. Nor are they comfortable in any of the existing transgender profiles described above. These may include feminine males who do not

# The Spectrum of Transgender Expression

identify as women, or masculine females who do not identify as men. Between the binary gender poles lies an infinite variety of personalities and presentations, allowing for individual mixes of masculine, feminine and gender-neutral elements. Many even consider themselves as **gender fluid** in that they can respond to changes in gender identity over time and in differing situations. As the binary sex-role system becomes less of a controlling factor in future people's lives, gender queer or gender fluid identities will likely become more widespread.

**Drag Queens and Drag Kings:** *part-time appearance and behavior change.* As mentioned previously, categories are dangerous things. Quite often drag queens and kings come from the gay, lesbian or bisexual communities and dress in "drag" (*see Glossary*) as caricatures or extreme presentations of the mainstream male and female sex-roles—often as celebrities. There is sometimes a performance element to these presentations, like a stage show of some kind, or they may simply be part of the crowd at a local club, blending in with a less flamboyant style. Some drag queens and drag kings do not consider themselves transgender, in the way that butch dykes (*see Glossary*) usually do not, but I will err to the inclusive side since drag kings and queens are both visible and noteworthy. I want to respect every person's classification of himself or herself, and in the end this is all about being *individual*.

Fortunately there won't be a pop quiz at the end of the book, so no need to memorize the above in detail. Rather the above distinctions are presented to give you an idea of how many variations exist—and these are but the general ones. I've created a table version of the these in Diagram 9 so that you can see the various factors involved in each expression form at a glance (*a sideways glance, that is*).

| Transgender Profile | Appearance Change? | Behavior Change? | Secondary Sex Change? | Primary Sex Change? | Full Time or Part Time |
|---|---|---|---|---|---|
| Crossdresser | Yes | No | Can | No | Part |
| Cogender (Bigender) | Yes | Yes | Can | No | Part |
| Transsexual | Yes | Yes | Yes | Yes | Full |
| Non-op/pre-op Transsexual | Yes | Yes | Yes | No/not yet | Full |
| Trans man, trans woman | Yes | Yes | Yes | Private | Full |
| Gender variant/queer | Can | Can | Can | Can | Either |
| Drag King/Queen | Yes | Yes | Can | No | Part |

Diagram 9: A Table of General Transgender Distinctions

# The Spectrum of Transgender Expression

**There's more: lots more.** When you start adding sexual orientation into the above mix, diversity is multiplied. You've probably heard terms like gender blender, stone butch, she-male, the list goes on (see *Glossary* for definitions of the above). Some are outdated terms, some are derogatory, some are so new that the graffiti paint isn't even dry yet.

Since it ultimately comes down to individual identities, it would become somewhat counter-productive to pile on more distinguishing characteristics here. But I have included a *Transgender Glossary of Terms* at the end of this book, which lists a number of different terms that hint at the diversity of identities all around us. It's compiled from many glossaries I've researched via the internet, is fairly up to date and something you're not likely to find in your local library quite yet: an interesting quick read. This will be kept relatively current on my web site **www.LearnAboutTransgender.org**.

**It's not about "the surgery."** As you can see, there is tremendous fundamental diversity in the transgender population, involving many combinations of mental and physical identity expressions. So this is a good time to make one issue very clear:

▼ **Surgery is NOT the defining factor of being transgender.**

One's true nature lies in one's core identity. If this identity falls outside the boundaries of a social binary sex-role, ***that*** is what defines someone socially as transgender. Genital Reassignment Surgery (previously termed Sex Reassignment Surgery) is a specific ***response*** to being a *certain type* of transgender person, a type that actually represents only one part of the diverse transgender population.

Some transgender people can become rather sensitive to questions involving so-called "lower surgery" (genital), often termed "***the*** surgery." This is because there has been altogether too much emphasis on genitalia, at the expense of the real issue: *identity*.

Just because someone is openly transgender, it doesn't mean it's open season for an invasion of privacy. The controversial nature of someone's identity should not overrule common courtesy: it's not likely you'd ask a woman you just met whether she's had a hysterectomy. There's a time and a place, that's all. (*TV talk show host's first question: "So have you had **the** surgery?" A reasonable TG guest response: "Well gee, sir, may I ask if you've been circumcised?"*)

**A further word on cross-dressing** is warranted here, since this phenomenon represents a fairly common thread that runs through so many transgender experiences. TGs are often driven by this mysterious desire to don the clothing and adornment of the other sex-role *long before they even know they are transgender*. We talked a little about this in the earlier section *Feelings: pathways around conditioning*. Cross-dressing is a very rewarding experience, either because it satisfies the needs of a core identity, or it gives sensual pleasure, or both.

Because cross-dressing is wearing the clothes of another *sex*, it has been historically thought that all cross-dressing is a form of sexual deviance or perversion.

▽ **Ultimately it doesn't matter whether cross-dressing is role-driven or fetish-driven, because these are both potentially healthy pursuits (as long as all civil rights are respected).**

It is our historical fear of and aversion to *sexual* issues, especially sexual diversity, that drives people to demonize cross-dressing as an "unhealthy fetish thing." Many people appropriately consider fetishes as gifts, "wired-in" sources of pleasure that might otherwise be hard to come by (*as it were*). As author and performer Kate Bornstein puts it, **consensual, considerate and non-harmful** sexual and fetish activities are a valid fulfillment of diverse human sexuality (my thanks to Kate for articulating this 3-part perspective).[25]

In many cases, cross-dressing does other than give a person sensual pleasure. It creates an opportunity to act out the *behavior* of the desired sex-role, since it is then socially consistent with the new appearance. In other words:

▼ **Cross-dressing can enable TGs to act out the social sex-role that corresponds to their core identity by aligning their outer appearance with their inner gender.**

**Welcome to the association.** It's easy to see how this would help *observers* to more easily accept someone who "looks the part," but why exactly does appearance seem to affect a TG's *own* ability to act out other genders?

One answer lies in early **associations** we all form as infants. We observe consistently that the people around us who *act* a certain way usually *look* a certain way. *We can form a strong and lasting association between appearance and behavior.* That is, we begin to recognize certain forms of social identity. So looking the part frees a transgender person to act out a gender identity while feeling consistent, inside and out. It's literally how TGs *see* themselves, and we usually see ourselves significantly by our external image. TGs describe this with the statement, "Now my outside matches my inside."

Again, it is very important to understand that cross-dressing is not necessarily a "stage" that transgender people progress through to an inevitable transsexual outcome. It is often a valid and lasting means of moving between gender roles to fulfill the needs of a certain core identity. Crossdressers are no less "serious" or "authentic" than, say, transsexuals or gender queers: each can be a completely appropriate response to a personal identity. And each has its own set of tough challenges.

**Confusing feelings, mistaken identities.** It is true that many male heterosexual cross-dressers can be sexually stimulated by their own feminine transformation. Since males who are defined as heterosexual are attracted sexually to females, it is reasonable that those who cross-dress could have a fetishistic response to their own feminine form while dressed as such. The same might occur for cross-dressing females.

It would be helpful for all of us to understand that a strong initial sexual response to crossdressing for many heterosexual males and females *can* be confusing to them, sometimes obfuscating what might essentially be an *identity* issue rather than a fetish one. When you *look* like the kind of person you're also *attracted* to, it makes sense that you'll "turn yourself on" at least a little.

If cross-dressing *is* driven by a transgender identity issue rather than a fetish, this sexual response to one's own form will usually diminish significantly over time to a level that could best be described—though colloquially so—by the phrase, "Damn, I look *good*!" Thus the sexual/fetish response *can* be a stage that some cross-dressers go through. Feeling quite good about one's appearance is something that many humans want to feel about themselves; whether that's defined as fetishistic or not ultimately is not the issue. The point is, as I will talk about in Part III, not to jump to any conclusion and "pigeon-hole" anyone out of fear, ignorance or prejudice about cross-dressing, fetishism or sexual orientation.

You might at some point in your ongoing research run across the term "autogynephelia" (*this ten dollar word is pronounced "otto-guy-nuh-FEEL-ya"*), which translates as *deriving pleasure from one's own female form* (the complete definition can be found in the Transgender Glossary at the end of this book). There is a goodly bit of controversy surrounding this term, and it's not really appropriate to jump into that fray in this overview. Diversity theories abound; the trick is to avoid applying any one of these to *all* trans people.

# The Spectrum of Transgender Expression

**It's all good.** As mentioned earlier, all forms or profiles of transgender expression are potentially appropriate and valid. Even the transgender population itself needs to be reminded that:

**▼ Every transgender path can be a valid journey to an individual goal of personal fulfillment, of self-actualization. No single transgender identity or manifestation is superior or more authentic than another.**

This fact can take a lot of initial angst out of the discovery that someone you know is transgender. You don't have to immediately suspect surgery, or a Jekyll and Hyde transformation, or loss of a relationship because this person is going to "completely change." We'll discuss this in more depth in Part III. Ultimately, being transgender is a very personal and individual thing. So:

**▼ The only way to find out what being transgender means to the person in question is to directly question that transgender person.**

Communicate. That's the best way to find out exactly how this person's unique transgender identity will affect the relationship you've had with him/her and will now continue to have with her/him (respectively, but not necessarily).[26] In most cases, transgender folks deeply sympathize with the difficulty many people face in trying to understand them. They will usually make considerable effort to help you to adjust: they ultimately want you to accept them (even if they challenge you at first), not feel alienated from them or put off by them.

**"Closeted," alter-ego, or "out."** If the stakes are just too high to reveal a transgender identity in any way, a TG will have to keep things completely under wraps. If a transgender person is only able to manifest this aspect of self in complete privacy, it is said that this person is "in the closet," or "closeted." Sometimes he or she carries this truth inside and never expresses it in any way: a sad exile from self, of sorts.

Sometimes closeted TGs will take greater and greater risks, venturing out into public cross-dressed or dressing in private with ever increasing frequency until they are finally "caught." Often this is a subconscious desire for this identity to be revealed, even against the conscious fears and wishes of the TG, because in truth ***we human beings usually need to share and affirm ourselves to other humans to feel truly fulfilled.***

Other TGs will incorporate a Core Gender and/or Sexual Identity into their lives by essentially creating a second social persona through which to experience and express it. These are the people who spend part of their lives in one sex-role (mostly in their birth-assigned one) and part in another role—an alter-ego of sorts. They are represented in part by the crossdresser and cogender populations described earlier, who create a second identity through which they can live out at least some facet of their core selves. They can establish a different name for themselves in this role, whole groups of friends and social circles—all completely separate and even secreted from their original friends and family.

Sometimes cross-dressing provides a satisfying balance between two roles, neither of which the TG wants to spend full time in. Or it might be a fulfilling fetishistic pursuit in itself. And sometimes it is a step towards a full-time identity change—it all depends on the *individual*, and each expression can be appropriately valid.

Some of the TGs who spend time in two roles can be very open about this: the word often used in the LGBTQ community is being "out." Although most are not yet allowed to come to their workplaces in their alternate role, many are "out" at home, to some friends, and sometimes even to individual co-workers.

**Deep stealth.** Once a *full-time* transgender person has made the move into a new social identity, he or she might soon be facing yet another dilemma. Most TGs want simply to be accepted as the people they've really always been, without the overriding issue of being "trans."

Yet many now find themselves having to keep a secret once again—this time about the past rather than the presence within—in order to avoid the prejudice most people hold toward trans men and trans women. This is called living in "stealth," keeping one's past out of the public domain (with the exception of close friends, family and/or partner).

When a TG establishes a completely new life—a new partner, family, job and so on—with no hint of a former identity revealed to *anyone*, this is called living in "deep stealth." It is an unfair and often very stressful compromise. As the transgender phenomenon becomes better understood, however, more TGs are refusing to live in deep stealth, choosing instead to risk prejudice for true acceptance.

If a TG's core identity essentially demands a full-time change into a new public identity, this TG must eventually reveal this fact publicly—or "out" themselves—and begin the process of changing over to a new identity. This process is called "transitioning:" from one *social* identity to another.

**A specific meaning of the term "transition."** When a transgender person moves from a previous sex-role to some other form of identity expression, this is called a ***transition***. The term *transition* has been most used by trans men and women who are making a permanent, usually public and often physiological change from one sex or sex-role to another. You will often hear them say, "After my transition . . ." meaning after they made their change from one social identity to another.

▽ **A transgender "transition" is the process of moving from one social identity to another, most commonly referring to a trans woman's or trans man's open change to a new sex-role.**

It can apply to *any* changeover, including those to non-conforming queer or gender variant expressions that lie outside any common sex-role boundaries. Most part-time gender expressions, such as crossdressers, don't use the word *transition* to describe their frequent changeover processes. So for the most part I will use "transition" when referring to full-time sex-role changes, as these present the kinds of family and workplace challenges that we'll talk about at length in Part III.

In the way of a footnote, there is a saying among trans men and women that: *"When you transition, everyone transitions with you."* This is a declaration of empathy on the part of these TGs, an understanding that a transition is not only a challenge and burden for her/him, it is such for *everyone* around that TG as well.

**Directions in role changes (transitions).** Most of us have been raised in a binary sex-role environment, and will probably continue to live in one as well because it is currently so pervasive. So it's likely that a significant percentage of transgender people will develop a core identity that's based one of the standard existing sex-roles as well. Those TGs who change from one established social sex-role to another do so in either of two directions: Male To Female (abbreviated MTF) or Female To Male (abbreviated FTM).

Since many TGs either can't undergo or choose not to have genital reassignment surgery, they are not moving between male and female *sexes* but more accurately between masculine and feminine *sex-roles* (genders). So ultimately these abbreviations are as follows:

• *MTF means either Male To Female or Masculine To Feminine,*
• *FTM means either Female To Male or Feminine To Masculine*
*—depending on whether there are physical treatments involved.*

Sometimes you will see the abbreviation M2F or F2M as well.

The fact that these abbreviations are somewhat flexible is actually a good thing, because being transgender is not just about genital surgery. These acronyms are a convenient way to state the general kind of transgender movement someone has made or is making, and that's pretty much all we need to know.

Even though the word "transgender" translates as crossing gender boundaries, many transgender people, especially the younger generations, don't actually cross from one binary role to another but instead identify a gender (or personality) somewhere in the middle. And since we spend our lifetime growing and changing, our gender can change with our increasing self-understanding.

Thus the term **gender-fluid** has come into increasing use, as mentioned earlier in the this section, meaning that people express different aspects of themselves at different times. If you think about it, we each act a little different around various people and situations. You're a different person in front of your boss, I'll bet, than you are in the full swing of a bachelor or bachelorette party (*unless it's your boss in the hot seat*). So some folks apply this fluid nature of personality to gender expression: it makes sense when you really think about it.

Since people are often curious about (or sometimes obsessed with) physiology issues, let's talk a bit about what various bodily treatments can and can't do for a TG—and how these shouldn't be THE big issue in how we regard transgender people.

## Changes to Physiology

**Responding to a core identity.** The real role of psychiatric and psychological therapy is to help each person accurately *discover* and confirm his or her own core identity for themselves, not to *change* it. Attempts to "cure" core identities in the past through a variety of sometimes shocking treatments (literally) have proven to be consistently unsuccessful.[27]

It's the mental health care provider's job to help a TG sort through complex and interconnected feelings and issues, to help confirm in what ways he or she is transgender, and then to aid that individual in deciding what appropriate responses can or should be pursued. These are very personal decisions, involving family, friends, jobs and financial means.

In very many cases, no medical treatments are desired or decided upon. Instead other issues such as disclosure to family, friends and co-workers, agreements with family to allow time in a desired gender role, and other arrangements are dealt with to respond to his or her unique core identity needs (or *to resolve gender dysphoria*, as the therapists would put it).

In other cases—especially those wherein there is a conflict with a TG's Core Sexual Identity—medical treatment options are reviewed, considered, and pursued to help resolve the dysphoria.

**Effective medical treatments.** As is indicated by the psychiatric diagnostic manual DSM-IV-TR:[23]

▼ A significant percentage of the transgender population has an appropriate need for a variety of medical treatments to resolve gender

# The Spectrum of Transgender Expression

**dysphoria: to help align the body and/or social role with the individual core identity.**

Time and again over the years it has been shown that when these TGs receive appropriate medical treatments, they now at least have an *opportunity* to achieve happy and productive lives that were otherwise not possible for them. I want to stress here that *these treatments do not solve the myriad OTHER problems that TGs must still face in life: they simply allow for the* **possibility** *of core happiness.*

This was certainly the case for me: I could never have transitioned publicly to my true self without facial feminization surgery (FFS), a virtual life-saver. (You can see its dramatic effect in the About the Author pictures at the end of this book.) My strong masculine facial features literally blocked my ability to see myself as the feminine person I am inside. What I consider the "miracle" of FFS (two 11-hour surgeries) made my outside identity—of which one's face is a *major* component—match my inner true one. I now see myself as I truly am, which profoundly better enables me to address the host of other challenges in life with which I still wrangle incessantly.

**A summary of medical options.** Again, medical treatments are a very individual matter. It is currently required that each TG spend time with skilled professionals in order to get written authorization for any medical treatments they might want (whether or not this screening process is arguably fair in the larger picture).[28]

Since many of these treatments produce irreversible results, the professional community has set up a system of international standards to assist in psychological screening and optimizing medical practices. If you are interested in learning more about the transgender International Standards of Care (ISOC), you can do so by visiting **www.WPATH.org**, the web site of the *World Professional Association for Transgender Health*.

Various medical treatments and procedures are chosen to satisfy the identity and role needs of each different TG. This little book is not the place to delve into these in great detail—I will leave it to you to pursue further research if you have more specific questions about transgender medical options. In any case I thought it would be helpful to at least list some of the significant ones here to give you a better idea of the kinds of significant treatments you might otherwise wonder about.

**Female to Male treatments**:
- Hormone Replacement Therapy (HRT), chiefly testosterone;
- Chest surgery: breast reduction;
- GRS for trans men: chiefly metoidioplasty or phalloplasty, and/or scrotoplasty.

**Male to Female treatments**:
- Hormone Replacement Therapy (HRT), chiefly estrogen;
- Electrolysis or laser treatments: permanent removal of facial and body hair);
- Facial Feminization Surgery (FFS): bone and/or soft tissue reconstruction;
- Scalp hair restoration: transplants or scalp advancement;
- Breast (and sometimes hip and fanny) augmentation;
- Orchiectomy: removal of testicles and consequent testosterone production (a cost alternative to GRS);
- GRS for trans women: vaginoplasty.

I will leave it to you to research more specifics on the GRS procedures I've named above. Typing any of the words ending in "-plasty" into an internet browser will allow you to get the depth of detail you might want (*I'd like to keep this book rated PG*).

As you can see GRS for trans women is more straightforward, involving a fairly standard procedure with minor variations. GRS for trans men involves several options due to the functional vs. sensate option that one must choose between, requiring personal choices as to which route satisfies each trans man's identity needs the best.

You've probably also noticed that the FTM treatment list is a bit shorter than the MTF one. One reason is that testosterone does a lot of the gender alignment work for trans men (such as voice pitch, facial and body hair congruence) that surgical treatments must instead do for trans women. Estrogen does not reverse such things as facial bone growth, facial hair, or original voice pitch—all of which are very strong masculine markers. TGs must deal with certain social aesthetic realities, such as the fact that generally speaking males with a feminine face are much more socially acceptable than females with highly masculine facial features: especially with regards to the presence or absence of facial hair.

Since there has always been a lot of speculation surrounding genital surgery, I'll make one thing clear here: the penis is not *removed* from male-to-female transsexuals. Rather it is disassembled and redistributed inside the pelvic area. So it's technically still there (sans testicles), just "rearranged" a bit. (*I thought you guys might want to know that: it's better than the thought of just "cutting it off"... and you can uncross your legs now.*)

Various treatments can affect both the body and the mind, especially *hormones* as described earlier in the *Power of Hormones* section. Another route for learning more about the various treatments of a friend or relative is by visiting the trans woman oriented site **www.tsroadmap.com** or the trans man oriented site **www.ftmi.org**. Wikipedia (www.wikipedia.org) also provides good overviews on various surgical procedures.

**"The" surgery**. Although generally speaking the concept of sex-change surgery is a provocative subject, we need to keep things in perspective. It would be helpful for everyone to keep in mind this important fact:

▼ **Surgery does not *make* anyone a man or woman, it can only *align* the body with the man or woman *already inside*.**

GRS stands for Genital Re*alignment* Surgery, not "General 'Re-personification' Surgery." This is hugely important, and sadly some TGs find this fact out the hard way (e.g. a trans woman discovering that, for example, GRS did not in fact deliver instant female behavior, appearance or public acceptance). Being transgender is all about the *core identity*, not any surgeries that are in *response* to it. It's our culture's relentless obsession with sex that keeps bringing genital surgery to the forefront. We need to de-emphasize the role of surgery and put it where it belongs (*in a room marked "Privates: Do Not Disturb."*)

**The mind needs a body.** At least this is true for human beings. And for some transgender human beings their brains need a certain kind of a body and will not truly rest until they get it.

▼ **For many a transgender person, the brain will never be satisfied until it can behave the way it wants, with the chemistry it needs, in the body with which it identifies.**

It is why the physical treatments described in this section can be so effective for certain transgender people, by giving the brain the environment for which it has developed such a fundamental need within the first two years of life (beginning with conception). It is also why, for one thing, trans men respond so well to testosterone, yet that same hormone conversely causes significant angst to trans women. And vice versa for estrogen. Through HRT each of these hormones benefit these people significantly by supplying the individual brain with the chemistry it wants.

Again, physiological treatments can effectively resolve the identity needs of many transgender people, but these do not address the host of *other* problems that will sometimes relentlessly dog most any human being throughout life.

In fact, ***undergoing these kinds of treatments, as part of a transition, can create a legion of* new *problems***: many of which we'll touch on in Part III—which is happening right . . . . . . . . *now*.

# III.

# Relating to Diversity

## Accepting a Transgender Truth.

**So what's new, exactly?** Just because a trans person's inner identity has been *hidden* for up to a lifetime doesn't mean it hasn't always been there. Even though a core identity *has* been there pretty much all along, many TG's are not consciously *aware* of it until well into life. While there are lots of reasons a transgender truth might have been withheld, one thing you should realize is this:

▼ **The inner truth of many TGs' core identity has been suppressed so deeply and so early in life that it has actually been hidden from the TGs themselves.**

The revelation that someone is transgender is probably more mutual than you might think; he or she may have simply discovered it a bit sooner than you did.

When you find out that someone you know is transgender, it feels like a sweeping upheaval—like that *person* has changed, not just your *knowledge* of a *part* of that person.

▼ **Remember that this person has *always been* transgender: this TG hasn't really changed, it's your *knowledge* of this part of him or her that has changed.**

We'll talk later on about why this *seems* to be such a comprehensive change, in the section entitled *New person or new role?*

**Feeling betrayed.** When someone you've known a long time reveals to you that he or she is transgender, it's hard not to feel somewhat betrayed, that this person just pulled a huge "one-eighty," has "held out on you" all this time. It will help you to shed this feeling if you can try to see things from the TG's point of view, by putting yourself in his or her shoes (*so to speak . . . I'm not asking you to cross-dress*).

So here are a couple of good questions and answers to stimulate some empathy on your part.

1) Why couldn't this person have divulged this much sooner; why wait all this time until now?

Answer: it's *fear*. Fear of the loss of the relationships that he/she *knows* will be at risk when the truth is revealed. Is it really fair to expect anyone to expose something that *he or she probably didn't even fully understand or work through all that long ago*? Transgender people are, after all, only human too. They are vulnerable, imperfect, needy and afraid of the unknown—just like you and, well, me.

2) How could we really expect anyone to expose in themselves what most people would regard as "sexual deviancy" without some guarantee from us that they will not be immediately judged and sentenced?

Answer: we shouldn't, and we need to put this in the forefront of our minds as soon as possible. We need to forgive people for being fearful human beings. We should not feel betrayed but rather *valued*. People only fear the loss of things they value: and that could be, for one, *you*. (Yes, you *should* blush.)

**Denying denial.** In the end, we all need to know that:

▼ **We can't choose the truth, but we *can* choose how to *deal* with it.**

That is the reality for transgender people and for everyone with whom they have relationships. No matter what, **the truth must be recognized, not denied**. Acceptance does not mean unconditional support, but it does involve recognizing the facts in this personal situation and at least *considering* these. We'll go into more specific ways to accomplish acceptance in the following sections.

It *is* unfortunate for *all* parties that anyone's transgender nature has been hidden, but: better late than never in the big picture. Once the truth is known and accepted as such, the work begins on how to *address* it—and the *how* is different for every single person. It is most certainly a serious challenge to sort through facts, feelings, assumptions and misunderstandings, but it can be done with mutual success if we have the patience and the compassion to work through new territories. And to try to *trust* in one another, to let the strength of a previous relationship enable the creation of a new one, wherever that takes each person.

**The value of an open mind.** Nothing will help you more to redefine and grow from a new transgender relationship than *opening your mind*. An open mind is a most critical asset in *all* things, for:

▽  **An OPEN MIND has nothing to lose and everything to gain. Conversely a closed mind has a lot to lose, and can cause others to lose a lot.**

Of all that you take away from this book, I hope that the above is high on your list. I believe that each of us can benefit a great deal by applying this basic attitude to *everything*, big and small, that we perceive and encounter from day to day. An open-minded approach to social interaction presents a wealth of personal enrichment that a closed mind will never discover. A Chinese proverb says, **"*A closed mind is like a closed book: it's just a block of wood.*"**

So the following sections present a number of relational perspectives and suggestions that can offer a world of new opportunities from which open minds can greatly benefit.

# Relational Shockwaves

Sorting through a lifetime's accumulation of complex personal identity issues and then deciding how to embrace these is a daunting task for *anyone*, to be sure. Dealing with the often traumatic *consequences* of revealing one's transgender nature to family, friends and co-workers is a whole additional bucket of rattlesnakes.

So it would help to talk about *why* people react the way they do to such news, so that eventually a lot of pain on all sides can be minimized and worked through more tolerably.

**Fear of the unknown**. Most people are initially reluctant to talk about transgender issues. One reason for this is our instinctive fear of the unknown, especially if that particular unknown is steeped in supposed sexual perversion or mental "disorder." It's very common for folks to respond to this news with "I've never *met* a transgender person before; so I haven't really *had* to think about it."

So it is understandable that you might be more than a little shocked to learn that someone you've known for some time turns out to be transgender. It may feel to you that this person has been hiding something for a long time, hasn't been honest, is not the person you thought you knew, has completely changed, and so on.

While these responses are understandable given the society within which we've been raised, they are not particularly constructive. So it would be helpful to remember this:

**It's very important to understand that it can take years for a transgender person to actually figure out what is going on inside well enough to even articulate it. And to divulge confusing and socially**

unfavorable inner sexual feelings is expecting a great deal of any human being.**

Again, put yourself in a TG's position if you can. If this were you, would you risk a valued relationship by spilling beans you don't even understand and are afraid to face up to in yourself? The stakes are very high: the social track record to date is that transgender divulgence creates a strong probability of the loss of relationships and jobs. So a TG must be extremely careful and *prepared* before breaking the news. This preparation takes even more time, sometimes years. *How careful would **you** be in packing your own parachute?*

**Part time sex-role changes.** If the TG in your life does not transition to a new *full-time* sex-role, you may not have occasion to see this person in another role. That depends on you and that TG and the situation involving his or her time in an alternate mode. Even so, just knowing that someone is transgender, even if for only part of the time, can put a bit of a "spin" on how you think about that person. Sometimes a knee-jerk reaction might be, "Wow, he/she is one of *those*!"

Again it is well worth your while to **reconsider** "one of those" in light of this **person** who you've actually *known* for a while. You have a golden opportunity to learn more about this transgender phenomenon by taking advantage of the real live "inside contact" you now have.

Ask this TG if you can meet for coffee, that you want to know more about this and would like to understand his/her point of view. Then just relax (*I know it's not that easy*) and listen. Ask questions and chew on the answers for a while. Give it time and keep it personable—you might be pleasantly surprised by how interesting and uplifting these talks can be. And you can take some comfort in the fact that you can begin to learn about transgender expression without having to actually witness it—if this thought is uncomfortable to you—through your part-time TG.

**New person or new role?** In every relationship that we have, this person that we know serves a *role* of some kind in our lives. Spouse, friend, relative: we've learned over the years to define certain relational roles, and we fit each relationship into a certain type. Pause for a moment and consider this:

▼ **The most fundamental relational classification we have in our society is whether it involves people within the same sex or between different sexes.**

In a binary society, friendships involving men with other men or women with other women (i.e. same-sex) enjoy certain freedoms and latitude. Any interaction *between* men and women, on the other hand, is fraught with sexual innuendo, questionable agendas, and a minefield of potential misinterpretations. For example, many heterosexual females regard a friendship with a gay male much differently than that with a heterosexual male: the former feels "safe" while the latter inherently possesses sexual "tension."

We almost always *classify* the relationship we have with someone—at a very fundamental or even subconscious level—based upon whether it is a *same-sex* or an *"opposite-sex"* one (there's that loaded "opposite sex" term again). This strongly influences what we can and can't do or say to that person. So it makes complete sense that when someone changes his/her sex-role on you, it's back to square one: you feel like you have to re-define the fundamental nature of that relationship from the ground up.

▼ **When transgender people change from one sex-role to another, this seems to topple the very nature of the relationship from the viewpoint of those who knew them before the change.**

"Boy howdy you've got *that* right!" you say. Nothing points this out more clearly than the ever-present *pronoun* issue. If I had a dime for every time someone tripped over a pronoun when referring to me early in my transition, I could buy a box full of my own books. This is *completely* understandable, because it takes a lot of time to switch this fundamental relational role in our heads after we've known someone as otherwise for such a long time. Some TGs get ruffled at the wrong pronoun, but it just shouldn't be such a big deal because it's so very understandable. (*I'm happy if someone just applies a clean word to me.*)

When a TG takes on essentially the "opposite" social *role* of the one in which we've previously associated him or her, we instinctively feel that this *person* has now completely and fundamentally changed; that the person we knew is "gone" and something foreign has now taken over (á la *Invasion of the Body Snatchers*). **It is a daunting challenge for a TG to prove that, on the contrary, "I'm still here! It's still me, though I may look different now."**

The fact is that most all of the perspectives, values, and character qualities that formed the basis of your relationship with that person are still there, alive and well. What's new is that many heretofore hidden qualities now *augment* the person that you've always known, while some of the previous sex-role-related characteristics are abandoned since these were socially mandated, not chosen naturally. But by and large—in spite of what your eyes might want to tell you—most of what makes this TG the person you've always known is still there.

▼ **We now see the *whole* person in a TG, not a completely different person, even though their appearance and social role may have changed significantly.**

I expressed it to people this way: **same book, new chapter, different cover**. A bit glib but fairly accurate.

# Relating to Diversity

Transgender people challenge us rather dramatically with the fact that **there is indeed a fundamental distinction between the person *and the* role**. We usually don't recognize this in our day-to-day familiar relationships.

**"Please just give me a chance."** It's one thing to consider intellectually that this is the same person, and quite another to look at the *woman* in front of you who used to be your touch football teammate and beer drinking buddy. That's a mind stretch that just plain doesn't come easily. It's hard to look past all the visual cues to see the old friend who is still there. It will take time, but *if you give it a chance it will very likely happen.*

It is helpful to try to understand that mannerisms, clothing, and speech patterns are all "trappings" of that person, they do not *define* him or her. The new facets you now see are the things that couldn't be expressed in a former role, because they weren't socially allowed and had to be hidden inside. There's a darn good chance that though she might not *play* football with the guys now, she still loves the game and would relish watching one any time with the gang, a large plate of nachos and plenty of beer.

The real tragedy is when friends or relatives refuse to even meet or talk with a TG once the truth is announced. This occurrence tends to call into question the true quality of that relationship from the point of view of the TG.

⚧ **There is a saying in the transgender population that when you transition, you find out who your real friends are.**

This is not always good news, but many TGs are reporting that old relationships have become deeper than ever after their real identity has been revealed. Many friends and relatives understand how risky and vulnerable it is to share such deeply personal information, and that this gesture can be very moving and encouraging for more closeness both ways.

**There is no substitute for a face-to-face meeting.** If there was any value in the relationship you've had with this TG, he or she deserves the respect of at least a brief meeting in person. You never know, it might pleasantly surprise you, or just be briefly uncomfortable at worst. (*And I don't mean the "uncomfortable" that a doctor claims just before placing something in you that nature never intended.*) You have more of a chance of getting a headache from this book than being harmed by a quick drink with your TG friend, relative or colleague. Really: think about it.

It might help you to prepare for such a meeting by watching other transgender people in action on some of the more recent non-sensational television programs and documentaries, such as *ABC 20/20, Oprah, Good Morning America, Larry King Live* and others. Some of these can be found on my web site **www.LearnAboutTransgender.org**, or perhaps your TG friend or relative can get recorded copies of interviews or recommend movies for you to watch.

If we've had a personal relationship with this person firsthand, that should at least carry enough weight and credibility for us to *reconsider* vague fears of an unknown issue and to make an effort to get a direct and personal look at it for ourselves.

☿ **To refuse a firsthand glimpse of this TG's viewpoint would be a needless loss of a relationship you once valued. It is very much worth the effort to reconsider what you thought you knew, or were afraid to learn, by talking face-to-face with someone you *do* know.**

Think about it this way: you have nothing to lose if you do, and potentially a *lot* to lose if you don't. If you've known this person for a long time, try to spend a *lot* of face-to-face time with him or her: ***the longer you've known someone in a previous sex-role,***

***the longer it will take you to "shift gears" in your mind and see this person for who they really are.*** Nothing will help more than personal interaction.

The remainder of Part III will *touch on* some of the basic kinds of relationships we have in our lives, to perhaps prime you to think about these and give you some very fundamental suggestions. Please remember that this is not a "how to" book and I am not a licensed therapist, just a transgender woman with a lot of experience to draw from. The few things I do talk about are meant to encourage you to move ahead into more research and learning about your specific relationship with a transgender person in your life.

# The Family

The most fundamental social unit that most cultures recognize is the immediate family. For a transgender person this can involve a spouse or partner, children, parents, and siblings. Before we discuss specific types of familial relationships, there is one universal question that is all too often emotionally raised after a transgender family member makes that difficult announcement.

**"How could you *do* this to us?"** This is a very revealing question. It strongly asserts that this TG has set out to actually *do* something to *others*. ***This question completely misses the point.*** What has really happened is that this person has decided to *be* who he or she really is. What this change "does" to others is really a matter of **how these others react** to this very personal decision—and the nature of each response is the choice made by each reacting person, *not* the TG.

Of *course* this decision affects a number of *other* lives as a result, but we must all be very clear that the underlying reason was almost certainly *not* to *do* damage to the family or to undo particular relationships. Any potential reactions from family members are *responses* to the TG's recognition of and commitment to an underlying identity that's always been there.

Most often a TG must decide to "come out" in spite of a truly gut-wrenching fear of what this might precipitate from various family members. Therapists spend lots of time making sure that TGs really know what's at risk. And yet many will ultimately decide to go ahead with this potentially costly step.

**It's a matter of *being*, not *doing*.** TGs' decisions to disclose this kind of news are driven by what they ARE, and what they must do about *themselves*. Once again, these aren't fundamental decisions to do something directly *to* anyone else. So a more appropriate form of the initial question would be, "Why are you doing this?" while leaving off the tempting addendum "to us." This focuses on the TG's personal reasons to disclose their true nature and to figure out where to go with that truth.

▼ **Transgender people reveal their true selves because it's who they ARE, not because they want to DO anything to anyone else. Instead of asking a TG "Why are you doing this *to us*?" it is far more appropriate to just ask, "Why are you doing this?"**

The answer to this more appropriate question will of course be unique to each TG, but perhaps the most universal underlying cause is, "Because I *have* to." Remember that we talked earlier in the *Brain Sex and Gender* section in Part I about how each individual brain can develop gender and sexual orientation independently from genitalia. This means that some people can have essentially a more female-type brain in a male body or a more male-type brain in a female body. And that ultimately such a TG's brain will never be happy until it can behave the way it wants, with the chemistry it needs, in the body with which it identifies.

As I mentioned at the end of Part II, transgender people desire very much to respond to and in many cases live out the identity that their brains have developed, whether this development is through nature or nurture it doesn't matter. If family and society require a behavior based largely on a body (sex) that differs significantly from a person's true identity, the stress can eventually be just too much for that TG to bear any longer.

So individual answers to the above question might be in the form of "because I just can't live a lie any more," or "this has been tearing me apart too long and I can't take it any more," or "I have nothing if I don't have myself," or "now that I understand who I really am, I just can't live another day without being my true self," or the scariest answer, "it's either this or suicide." All are variations of the fundamental need or overwhelming desire to live out a true identity.

So really *it's more a question of what each family member will do to the TG after the news*. And I must sadly report to you that one of the tragic things families all too often do to transgender members is to cast them out. Having been a spouse, a parent and a sibling, the very *thought* of this tears at my heart. Two truly lovely trans women friends of mine each were ostracized from their families after their transition. One of these eventually committed suicide, a terrible loss for which I still weep to this day. No one should *ever* have to choose between self and family. (See *If Your Child Might Be Transgender* further on in this book for some underlying reasons why this can, unfortunately, happen.)

**Pulling together.** At a time when transitioning TGs really need support from family and friends, it is instead all too often a time of relational crisis for them, leaving them to rely on people outside the family for real support. This is an extremely debilitating situation, one that taxes most TGs to their limits and sometimes, tragically, beyond.

Instead this should be a time to *pull together as a family*, not go on the defensive or on the attack. It would make everyone more constructively compassionate to remember in their hearts that this transgender family member very likely *does* indeed love and cherish the family, is torn between two vitally important forces, and that in the end a TG's need to be true to self outweighs everything.

Now let's focus on more specific types of relationships and some of the issues that these can involve.

# Intimate Partners

One of the most treasured relationships we can experience is between intimate partners. The most common such partnership is marriage, but in order to include such alternatives as common law relationships I will use the term "partner" as well as "spouse." Much of this section will apply to most any type of intimate or committed relationship.

In this section I will present some observations and insights regarding intimate couples dealing with a newfound transgender issue. These perspectives are borne out of my own experience, many personal interviews, and years of research. I have both been *in* intimate relationships (including marriage with one child) in which I was eventually compelled to reveal my transgender truth, and I have also personally known of or been closely *involved* in such relationships through transgender friends of mine.

For example, I had the most profound experience of watching a divorce happen right before my eyes, during an evening of soul-baring between a married couple (where one partner recently announced a transsexual identity), myself and another close mutual friend. So I am offering to you much that I've learned from this and many other personal experiences. (Remember, the following is no substitute for obtaining qualified professional support if that is appropriate for you in your own situation.)

**"What is this going to do to our marriage (or partnership)?"** This is a common and *very* appropriate response to learning of a partner's transgender nature. But as is the case with any challenge in life, *the worst thing we can do is to panic*. Fear can be either a motivator or an inhibitor, depending on how we react to it. Any permanent decision made hastily out of fear is very likely to be a damaging one to both parties. *The powerful urge to jump to conclusions can be nearly overwhelming.*

Emotions are real, and are inherently neither good nor bad as we discussed earlier. It's how we *react* to them that can be good or bad for us or others. We need to recognize our emotions, yet not let them take over or blind us from a constructive process.

▼ **Experiencing a transgender revelation is the beginning of a *process*, one that will take time to absorb, time to sort out, and time to work through to the most mutually beneficial outcome.**

Like the stages of grief (please refer to one example of a grief model provided at the end of this section), we each need to go through a personal series of emotions, in our own order and in our own time. Again, try not to make lasting decisions from initial emotional responses; rather give each other time to process each step in this important challenge of relational coping.

**We can't do this alone**. The transgender phenomenon touches just about every aspect of our lives and the society in which we live. *Coping with a transgender truth is simply too much for virtually ANY partnership to handle* on its own.

▼ **By far the most critical first step for intimate partners dealing with transgender issues is to obtain qualified professional therapy, for each partner and/or as a couple as the needs may be.**

The last decade has witnessed tremendous psychological and medical progress in understanding the transgender perspective on identity, and the many challenging issues that are involved. There are an increasing number of qualified transgender-knowledgeable

# Relating to Diversity

therapists—psychologists, psychiatrists and licensed counselors—who can provide critical help in sorting through a very complex and emotionally charged situation. An objective eye and some experienced guidance are very important tools to help a couple work through this process to the greatest benefit of *both* parties.

**Preparing to work things out.** There are a number of important qualities in any relationship that, if embraced from the beginning, can greatly help both partners through this process. *Some* of these are offered here, and more can be pointed out to you individually by your therapist(s).

**Trust**: this is a big one. In many cases the partner of a TG will initially feel betrayed by this new knowledge. This is when it is critical to understand that as imperfect human beings we often do the wrong things for the right reasons; or simply just don't understand what's going on inside well enough to even *begin* to articulate it; or are gripped into muteness by the specter of losing the very person we cherish most in life—our partner—because of the confusing and sometimes scary things going on inside.

▼ **Regardless of what it might feel like, it is critical that both parties embrace the concept that no one is *trying* to hurt anyone; in fact it is almost always just the opposite.**

Many transgender people earnestly believed throughout their lives that an intimate partnership and family would "correct" the confusing feelings inside, that these desires haunting them have just been misplaced sexual drives. The many ways that TGs try to outrun, deny or avoid the truth inside are staggering to realize.

Before discovering their core identities, many TGs born

male take on extremely dangerous situations and careers trying to prove their prescribed masculinity to society and to *themselves*. They join military special forces, take on high risk activities, you name it. Yet many of these "macho" men will readily admit that stepping publicly into a female role was the hardest and scariest thing they've done in their entire lives (*I can relate to that one*). Think about how much this says about the strength of social sex-role pressure.

So a lifetime of secrecy is not so much an issue of *trust* as it is a matter of deep and appropriate *fear*. Understanding this will help a partner to regain a feeling of trust from someone who has indeed been loving though humanly imperfect.

**Compassion**. This is hard for *both* partners to give, at a time when personal defensive emotions are so intense. It's not helpful to try to determine who has it better or worse, it is just *different* for each and uniquely difficult. Some folks keep very strong feelings held inside, others express them with emphasis; so the *apparent* strength of a feeling is not a good indication of it's actual power of influence. Emotions are not something that can be objectively quantified, and comparison is just not at all helpful to the process (as aptly put by the phrase "comparison is odious").

▼ **The more that each partner can look past his or her own feelings and consider how the other sees this situation, the better will be the communication and the possibility of considerate resolution.**

*Effective communication requires real listening.* That means focusing on the other's point of view when he or she is speaking. It's critical that the transgender person comprehend the magnitude of the shock a partner can experience on learning of something that can turn an entire world upside down. The TG has probably been living with this thing one way or another for years. The partner, however, often gets blind-sided in one fell stroke: it can feel like life's rug has been pulled abruptly out from under the partner's feet, and the feeling of vertigo can be devastating. The TG needs to keep this in mind constantly, every step of the way.

Pausing to actually *feel* how deeply frightening it is for a transgender partner to reveal a confusing inner dilemma can very much help to allay any initial feelings of betrayal and loss of trust. What we each do is one thing, but *why* we do it—or don't do it as the case may be—is very important. Yes, the doing or not doing of the thing can hurt, but if the *why* is sincere and without ill will, it is beneficial to keep this in mind. *Being transgender is something one* **is**, *not a misguided choice such as an extra-marital affair.*

**Respect**. If partners consistently make an effort to consider each other's perspective compassionately, it better enables each to *respect* the needs of the other and not emphasize either party's issues excessively. We can give each other respect by:

• Allowing lots of *time* for the TG's partner to work through things, even though that TG may be dying to move ahead toward his or her own long-suppressed identity.

• Allowing the TG time with transgender friends for support and compassion that just can't be had at home right now, understandably. This is not abandonment, it is simply a fundamental need for empathy and support.

• Honoring the specific therapy needs of *both* partners. Many partners of TGs fear that transgender specialists are really advocates of the transgender cause, will not consider the marriage/partnership objectively, and will try to "convert" or pressure them into the transgender mind-set.

Even though many transgender-experienced therapists are skilled in family and partnership issues, it is important to respect the desire of a partner to get *individual support from a therapist outside of transgender circles*. This can be seen by that partner as a greater potential for unbiased empathy.

**Openness.** It is very difficult for each partner to stay open when on the defensive, when both parties feel potentially threatened by this situation in one way or another. When facing potential loss, it is somewhat instinctive for us to grab onto our position tightly and to close our minds to any other options. This is *never* a good thing, and here's why.

▼ **Maintaining an open mind is the key to discovering and considering *all* options, some of which might be much better than the one we had instinctively been defending.**

Temporarily considering another perspective or suggestion *is not an act of capitulation*. Each person still retains the right to make a final decision according to his or her own desires and needs, either old or new. *But it's a much better-informed decision.* Consider everything and everyone seriously. Neither party has anything to lose by doing so, and moreover a lot to gain.

**The person vs. the role.** We talked about this a little earlier, but an intimate partnership can present a more difficult challenge in distinguishing between the person and the *role* of that person in a relationship. In most cases, we need both: we need certain important *roles* in our lives to feel complete, and we also fall in love with a very individual *person* for a number of reasons. When a transgender truth is revealed in an intimate relationship, both of these relational aspects are hit hard—but it helps to keep these distinct when weighing all of the feelings and options.

You and your partner each need important roles filled: husband, wife, partner, significant other, soul-mate, father, mother, and so on. Each of you has a very clear idea of what a partnership and family is supposed to look like, and what roles are required to make it all happen. When a partner comes out as transgender, the whole role structure seems to fall apart: one has to re-think everything.

It's not just a matter of what each partner needs, it's also a matter of how the partnership will be regarded by others. This is a big deal, let's face it. Questions like, "What will my family/church/friends think of me now?" or statements like "I'm not lesbian!" pop up immediately and strongly. Remember, so much of our sense of self lies in our Social Identity, probably more than we realize; it's challenging to look past this and to focus on core values.

As far as core values go, what *is* the role of sexual intimacy in the relationship? Suddenly sexual orientation may be turned upside down. Does a change in gender or sex affect your ability to focus on the person you know and love who is still there? Does intimacy require sexual intercourse? Is physical affection other than intercourse still possible? What is it exactly that you love in this person? Does a soul have a sex? This is very challenging stuff, the kind that begs for introspection, counseling and support from all quarters.

There is an aspect of what I will call true love that holds the happiness of your partner nearly as precious as your own, with relatively few conditions. In spite of the degree of challenge and the intensity of emotions that will run their course, if both parties can hold on tight to the concept of friendship, based in true love, it will work wonders for the eventual outcome.

The relationship will indeed change: the only constant in life, after all, is change. But even if you must go your separate ways, try to do so in peace and love—at least in a friendship love. I know many couples that have done so: it is entirely possible and even probable if you have the patience, compassion and open mind to see this thing through. If you truly cared about each other, you can continue to do so even if you decide to no longer live together.

**Similar partnership challenges.** There are other kinds of challenges to a partnership that are more purely medical in nature; considering these might open up avenues for support and general perspectives on coping. Partners are hit with paralyzing strokes, Alzheimer's, debilitating accidents, cancer, MS, Lupus, so many things that can topple the family role structure and the intimacy you can maintain with a partner. You probably know someone who's been through something like this—I myself have, more than once. Your therapist will point out some of the common threads that run through these relational blows. I point out these medical parallels to help you realize that the kinds of challenges you face are not limited to transgender disclosure, and in fact happen all around you.

**The stages of grief.** At the beginning of this section I mentioned the existence of the Stages of Grief models. There are many versions to be found these days: one of the earliest is the Kubler-Ross Model as proposed by Elizabeth Kubler-Ross in her book "On Death and Dying" published in 1969. Her model is comprised of 5 stages:
1) Denial
2) Anger
3) Bargaining
4) Depression
5) Acceptance

This model suggests the order in which these emotions usually take place, but the *actual* order and intensity of each stage can vary significantly from one individual to another.

There is another model, involving seven stages, that in my opinion seems a bit more suitable for people coping with the loss of *others*. I've included one version of this model as shown on

**www.recover-from-grief.com.** It is displayed here (though slightly modified) for your convenience but I encourage you to visit this site and others like it. I have taken the liberty of editing the original text to make it more appropriate for a transgender situation, by ~~striking through~~ death-specific references and adding in *italicized terms* for clarity (with my sincere thanks to the hosts of this valuable site).

1. SHOCK & DENIAL - You will probably react to learning of the ~~loss~~ *transgender truth* with numbed disbelief. You may deny the reality of the ~~loss~~ *news* at some level, in order to avoid the pain. Shock provides emotional protection from being overwhelmed all at once. This may last for weeks.

2. PAIN & GUILT - As the shock wears off, it is replaced with the suffering of unbelievable pain. Although excruciating and almost unbearable, it is important that you experience the pain fully, and not hide it, avoid it or escape from it with alcohol or drugs.

    You may have guilty feelings or remorse over things you did or didn't do with your loved one. Life feels chaotic and scary during this phase.

3. ANGER & BARGAINING - Frustration gives way to anger, and you may lash out and lay unwarranted blame for the ~~death~~ *situation* on someone else. Please try to control this, as permanent damage to your relationships may result. This is a time for the release of bottled-up emotion.

    You may rail against fate, questioning "Why me?" You may also try to bargain in vain with the powers that be for a way out of your despair ("I will never drink again if you just bring him back").

4. "DEPRESSION", REFLECTION, LONELINESS - Just when your friends may think you should be getting on with your life, a long period of sad reflection will likely overtake you. This is a

normal stage of grief, so do not be "talked out of it" by well-meaning outsiders. Encouragement from others is not helpful to you during this stage of grieving.

During this time, you finally realize the true magnitude of your ~~loss~~ *situation*, and it depresses you. You may isolate yourself on purpose, reflect on things you did with your ~~lost one~~ *partner*, and focus on memories of the past. You may sense feelings of emptiness or despair.

5. THE UPWARD TURN - As you start to adjust to *a new* life *with or* without your dear one, your life becomes a little calmer and more organized. Your physical symptoms lessen, and your "depression" begins to lift slightly.

6. RECONSTRUCTION & WORKING THROUGH - As you become more functional, your mind starts working again, and you will find yourself seeking realistic solutions to problems posed by *a new* life *with or* without your loved one. You will start to work on practical and financial problems and reconstructing yourself and your life *with or* without him or her.

7. ACCEPTANCE & HOPE - During this, the last of the seven stages in this grief model, you learn to accept and deal with the reality of your situation. Acceptance does not necessarily mean instant happiness. Given the pain and turmoil you have experienced, you ~~can~~ *may* never return to the carefree, untroubled YOU that existed before this ~~tragedy~~ *disclosure*. But you will find a way forward.

You will start to look forward and actually plan things for the future. Eventually, you will be able to think about your ~~lost~~ loved one without pain; sadness, ~~yes~~ *perhaps*, but the wrenching pain will be gone. You will once again anticipate some good times to come, and yes, even find joy again in the experience of living.[29]

Even though models such as the above were created to deal with the loss of a loved one through death, there is potential benefit to you and yours in that these articulate a *process* of dealing with the revelation of a transgender identity in your partnership. Again, remember that individual experiences may vary significantly from these models, but they underscore the fact that we all engage in a process that takes time and patience to get through.

## Transgender Disclosure to Children

**"What do we tell the kids?"** Initially it feels like it will *never* be a good time to tell a child about such a complex and potentially upending situation as revealing the transgender identity of a parent. Each family is different, each child is unique, and everyone needs to work through a good strategy for the best *long term* solution. Step #1 is: **consult a qualified therapist before you do anything else.**

**The role of a good therapist is critical to this process**. Your therapist(s) will help you to assess the capability of each child to deal with the news based on age, history with each parent, and emotional stability. Trust qualified therapists to help you understand the potential flexibility of young minds to adapt, and to assess each child's ability to cope—or not—with your unique situation.

**Your attitude makes a big difference**. There are a few universal observations about children that are worth mentioning in this section. One of the first things to think about when preparing for disclosure is that:

**▼ Children of all ages (including full-grown) are very much influenced by the attitude of each parent.**

When a toddler takes a moderate spill during play, for example, the first thing he or she usually does is *to look to a parent to see how to react to their own shock*. If the parent's response is easygoing and uplifting, the child will likely shrug it off and get back to playing. If the parent responds with alarm and angst, the child will almost certainly begin screaming.

The same holds true when presenting the family's transgender situation to children of any age. They will pick up on stress, disapproval, bitterness, patience, compassion or a positive outlook. ***Think hard about the non-verbal message you want to send to your children, because you WILL send one.***

If both partners can send a message of love for each child, and constantly exude a desire to *work this all out as a family*, it will significantly enable a positive and trusting attitude in your children through which real progress can be made with minimal stress. ***Keep telling your children out loud throughout this process that you love them no matter what.***

**Don't underestimate the perceptiveness and intelligence of children.** They're probably more aware than you think, *even if they don't show signs of it*. They may not know exactly what is happening, but more often than not they will pick up cues that *something* is going on. I don't know how many times I've heard from transgender friends that their children knew a lot more a whole lot sooner than they, as parents, suspected.

**▼ Children deserve as much respect as adults, and should be given credit for being a lot smarter than most people think they are—especially at a very young age.**

Remember, kids don't merely hear the words we speak, they read how we *feel* about what we are saying to anyone. They can key very perceptively off our small body language cues and tone of voice, perceiving a "change of atmosphere" in the household through parents' non-verbal cues.

It can be very difficult to cover our own emotions sufficiently enough for our children to make their own unbiased decisions; in the courtroom this influence is called "leading the witness." So each parent should take care to work through issues sufficiently—with the help of a therapist—so that any underlying feelings won't undermine a constructive message being conveyed to each child. Remember, *prejudice is something that is largely **taught** to children.*

If either party honestly has doubt as to whether they or the other parent can present transgender information with sufficient neutrality, it is all that much more important to consult with a therapist—ideally one that has experience with children *and* transgender issues. In any case, consult your therapist(s) and/or a child psychologist ***before*** you confront the children—and *be realistic*: with yourself and the therapists. Prepare yourself carefully before you approach each child. This is especially true for the transgender parent: *just because you feel better about yourself doesn't mean a child will feel better about you, so don't assume this.*

**If you think you can hide things from a child** for very long, think very carefully. Children can read that they are being talked down to, put on the spot, loved, ignored, brushed off, or treated evasively. Just because they don't ask doesn't mean they don't perceive that something is amiss.

In some cases your therapist might recommend that you DO withhold revealing a transgender situation for some period of time—sometimes years—and will suggest ways in which you can most successfully do so. It's not easy but it *can* be done with good advice: I can tell you this from my own personal experience.

**It's *when*, not *if*.** Another thing to consider is to ***take great care when yielding to a parental instinct to "protect" a child from an "inappropriately sexual" situation.*** Withholding of the truth, with the intent of avoiding a stressful experience at present, can backfire years later when that child *does* learn the truth and possibly feels betrayed by you for not having been told. Again, consult a qualified therapist as soon as possible.

▽ **Revealing a potentially observable transgender identity to the family is not a matter of IF, it is a matter of WHEN.**

As with every other aspect of dealing with a transgender disclosure, it is wise to *think in the long term* and make your decisions accordingly.

**Do your homework**. With a little research you can locate web sites, organizations and even local parents who have dealt with a transgender disclosure in the family. Two organizations I would highly recommend are:

**Gender Spectrum Family** at **www.genderspectrumfamily.org/**,
and
**Trans Youth Family Advocates** at **www.imatyfa.org/**.

And finally, I personally encourage you to *muster up a positive attitude*: **believe** that it is very possible for a transgender truth to be presented successfully to your children sooner or later. By and large kids are very flexible and adaptable, especially if you give them the constant clear message that *no matter what you love them*. Say it out loud, a *lot*. There are ever increasing accounts of greater parent-child closeness (to both parents) after a transgender situation is worked through. I am happy to say that this is the case with me and my son—so take heart: I'm here to tell you that it *can* be done.

## If Your Child Might Be Transgender

**If you observe cross-gender behavior from your child,** this is a whole different ball game than that of the preceding section. Of course I strongly recommend that you see a therapist who specializes in transgender children before you take *any* action with your child. At the same time I highly recommend reading the book *The Transgender Child* by Stephanie Brill and Rachel Pepper, ISBN 978-1-57344-318-0.[30]

The internet provides some great resources to help you assess your situation. Two that I recommend, once again, are Gender Spectrum Family, on the web at **www.genderspectrumfamily.org**, and Trans Youth Family Advocates at **www.imatyfa.org**. These kinds of sites can provide valuable resources for families with transgender members.

**A case against prohibition.** To give you something to think about, I will convey a *general* viewpoint regarding cross-gender expression in young children. ***Most therapists trained in gender issues recommend that you NOT prohibit outright a child's display of transgender behavior at home with family***, for many reasons. If it's an experimental phase of gender exploration then it will pass and he or she may resume a more cisgender/cissexual childhood. A qualified therapist trained in gender issues will help you determine whether or not it's appropriate to let the child continue exploration, with a clear set of boundaries.

If time reveals that it's *not* just a phase, then any suppression of these expressions could lead to serious problems that can haunt your child through adulthood (as was my own case). The suicide rate for suppressed transgender identity is alarmingly high, so consider whether you want to take this risk with your child if you are driven to dissuade him or her from transgender behavior "for their sake."

Yes, it's daunting and even heartbreaking to think about what your child might suffer displaying transgender behavior in school and at play. But many organizations are working very hard to pave the way for these kids, through protective legislation and educational programs all over the country. Take heart, you will not be alone in this, and there is *much* support to be had if you look for it.

**Some parent-to-parent comments.** I'm going to take this opportunity to share with you some perspectives I've received from other parents and gained from my own experience as one, and a good deal of time as the *only* one, to my son.

- **Each child's true personal happiness is our real priority.** While this would seem quite commonsense, I've observed that there exists a tendency for some parents to overlook much of a child's own inner identity and personal values in the rearing process. That is, they want their kids to be happy ultimately on *the parents'* terms, not on the *child's* terms. Let me explain.

Recognizing and honoring our children's personal values is often neither intuitive nor easy *if they differ significantly from our own.* **And since we humans are indeed individuals, our children will** *be different from us: it's just a matter of degree.*

As parents we have the right to raise our children "properly" by instilling in them the values that *we* embrace, **but only to a point**: without sufficient consideration of each child's unique personal perspectives, needs, interests, passions and identity, an approach of total parental control *can* be counter-productive in the long run. *This is especially true in a situation involving a gender-variant child.*

Therapists speak a lot about "boundaries" in relationships, and such a boundary exists when it comes to parental *guidance* versus *control*. It's not our child's job to "make us proud" by satisfying *us* according to our values and opinions on success and happiness. Rather:

▼ **It is our job as parents to help each child discover and develop their own values, who they are and what they want to do with their lives: and to do so with as little real harm as realistically possible.**

The issue is *their* survival, health and happiness, not ours; this is our real priority.

As mentioned earlier, it is always critical to learn and accept the truth; suppressing any truths in a child is a recipe for future disaster. The reason this is so likely is that *a* **suppressed truth cannot be addressed**. A transgender child may not be what we had in mind, but sometimes it's the truth. To reject a child based on an immutable truth is a needless and destructive tragedy for all concerned—and rejection comes in many forms, from suppression to exile.

When perspectives differ significantly, support can be difficult it's true. A family is the last bastion of acceptance and support that a child should be able to count on, especially if they are "different." Real love spans differences, both physical and mental, and there is no more important place for real love than in the family. They say "charity begins at home," and this goes for tolerance as well.

• **Keeping an eye on independence day.** A child may "toe the line" while living at home, then re-adjust or even rebound entirely according to his or her own values *as soon as he or she becomes independent*—which is, in most cases, inevitable. The problem is that this young adult is then unleashed to experiment without the support, guidance and appropriate boundaries maintained by loving and experienced advisors: parents.

The certainty of a child's eventual independence is a good reason to *know each child's innermost nature and desires while he or she is living at home*, where we can be of formative and appropriately protective value to his or her pursuit of happiness. Some kids need a lot of encouragement to reveal their feelings and desires, so **we must make an effort to draw these out**.

• **Children deserve a voice that is heard.** I'm sure we all agree that the prime directive of parents is to keep our children as safe as possible from harm, both physical and psychological. This is where our experience comes in: we can pass along very important lessons and *tools* to our children to help them avoid as much harm as possible.

So it *is* important to raise children according to parents' constructive values, yet it is even *more* important to realize this:

▼ **Children are much more likely to accept and embrace parental values and regulations if it's made consistently clear that each child is heard, respected and involved in the process: that he or she ultimately has a choice in behavior and must accept the reasonable consequences of each choice.**

The wrong choice can produce undesirable results for the child, especially in physical safety issues, so it is important that underlying reasons be clearly understood and strict boundaries agreed upon.

A child's consistent realization that he or she *has a say* in most things can often preclude internal alienation from and eventual rebellion against the very values being imposed upon them by parents. If a child sees consistently that he or she is *heard* and *considered*, accepting limitations is much more palatable—based on more objective reasoning than the dreaded "because I said so" (which is a clear way of saying "your viewpoint doesn't matter to me in the least" or worse yet "you're too stupid to think for yourself"). Children are smart and perceptive, but they are sensitive, too; a formative ego can be particularly fragile and defensive when it feels put down or brushed off. Affirming a child's intelligence when setting boundaries paves the way for much more responsible behavior.

• **Maintaining a healthy balance.** Balance is at least as important in a child/parent relationship as it is in a child's diet. While some parents may tend to be over-controlling with their children, others can be far too permissive with them—*which can be every bit as damaging as the former*. I have observed that **children without boundaries are almost always very unhappy children**. Kids *need* boundaries even though they ostensibly resist these, and will push and push until they find them. There is, in fact, important *security* that a child experiences in knowing boundaries and limits, and it is our duty to provide these with care and respect, but with *consistency* as well.

The word "balance" is one of the most important in my own vocabulary, and it applies to almost all aspects of life—most certainly to something as precious as children. An effective balance of control is most likely to be achieved and maintained through a dynamic *partnership* between each parent and child.

• **The parent/child partnership.** I personally think of parenting as a *partnership* with each child. Being openly considerate of a child's values leaves little opportunity for him or her to blame a parent for not having the unfettered freedom he or she usually wants.

▽ **The birth of a child is really the beginning of a partnership—not a dictatorship—formed between parent and child. Children are indeed the junior partners, but they deserve to have a voice in every choice, with the parent(s) having the final word—in some cases with professional consultation.**

I feel it is a parent's duty to make an open, considerate and consistent effort to understand a child's identity and values; then work out a process *together* toward his or her eventual independence while supplying the boundaries and limitations that are crucial to that child's balanced growth. And this becomes an even more critical issue with transgender children.

• **Knowledge is key to good growth.** If cross-gender behavior is a "phase" of identity exploration that a child wants to experiment with, *your knowledge of that child's innermost values and traits will help you decide on the best way to deal with this situation*—along with advice from a qualified therapist.

If it turns out that this behavior is *not* a phase, then it is even more important that you make an effort to draw out your child's inner values and to consult with an experienced *transgender-adept* professional.

As a parent I know how strong our sense of protection is for our children. But there IS such a thing as *over*-protectiveness; and sometimes we can do more harm than good by isolating children from tough issues rather than dealing with these as a parent/child partnership (involving a qualified therapist as necessary). In working *with* them we give children the *tools* they need for this and a host of future challenges that lie ahead in adult life.

Addressing the truth of a transgender child is one of many difficult processes that we must undertake as parents, involving nerve-racking risks and frustrating compromises. I, too, abhor the fact that we must often choose the lesser of two "evils" rather than the better of two goods. But I do believe it is best to constructively *address* (rather than deny) gender-variant behavior and other challenges dynamically as a parent/child partnership, and to negotiate the safest and most productive process for the best *long-term* returns—one day at a time.

## Friends and Relatives

**Be open to a very personal story.** Of all the whys and wherefores explained throughout this book, perhaps the most important overall recommendation is to *keep an open mind about what it means and doesn't mean for your particular friend or relative to be transgender.*

Again, being transgender is a *very individual thing.* He or she is still essentially the same person you've always known, but has demonstrated the honesty to share with you uniquely personal parts that need to be lived out.

**Before you decide in your mind what being transgender will do to the relationship, allow your TG friend or relative to personally show you or tell you what it means for him or her. Only then can you begin to determine to what degree you can accept or support an ongoing relationship.**

Keep an open mind and a positive attitude: try not to jump to any conclusions before you get specific information. And give yourself *time* to work through something new to you.

In some cases, being transgender means he or she will spend only part of the time in an alternate role and you may never see him or her this way. "Why did he/she bring it up, then?" you ask. Why not just continue the secrecy? Because secrecy *feels* wrong for most TGs, making their nature seem unacceptable and unmentionable. As we talked about earlier, we human beings usually need acceptance by others to feel real fulfillment, and this motivates us to share the things that are important to us with those whom we care about.

In other cases there is a full-time social role change for the TG, sometimes involving medical treatments that can significantly alter his or her appearance. Knowing this can initially daunt you from wanting to meet him or her face to face after these sometimes dramatic changes. But think about this next paragraph.

**Person to person: you owe it your relationship**, and to *yourself*. Before you decide how "weird" this might be, give your friend or relative the minimal respect of spending at least a few minutes with him or her *face to face*: for lunch or a cup of coffee. Most full-time TGs report that these personal meetings allow folks to see firsthand how good they feel in their own skin: ***happiness is something most people wear well.*** You can only perceive this kind of thing face-to-face: a phone call or email is no substitute.

▼ **Meeting face-to-face with your transgender friend or relative is very powerful in helping you re-define this person in your mind.**

Think of it this way: what's the worst that can happen? No one's going to bleed from it. If you meet and just can't handle it, say so politely and then give yourself time to think about it on your own for a while. Talk with mutual friends, get more input. Few things worthwhile come easily, and this is no exception.

If, after carefully considering this option, you just can't bring yourself to meet in person, then please at least do the following.

**If it's just too much for you right now, *say* so.** If you find yourself completely stalled at the thought of meeting with this transgender friend or relative in person, at the very least **do the honor of *telling* him or her you just can't make the leap.** Do it in writing if a phone call is too daunting. We are all human, and your TG friend or relative will probably try hard to understand even though it does hurt.

▽ **It is especially hurtful when transgender people tell friends or relatives and then never hear from them again, leaving these TGs feeling literally abandoned without a word.**

Separation without closure is just plain inconsiderate and the pain of it lingers indefinitely. A short letter or email would help a lot, and can bring a sense of closure important to both of you. *Accept one another's perspective and move on in peace.*

As a trans woman who transitioned relatively late in life, I have a lot of friends who knew me for decades in my former sex-role. I've maintained a lot of compassion for these friends: I know how hard it is to re-define a relationship that has spanned the sex-role chasm. This compassion has allowed me to accept someone telling me that they just can't deal with my transition: but only if they have the minimal common courtesy to tell me so at least in writing and in a remotely considerate time frame. It takes, what, 5 minutes to write and send an email?

*For a trans person, no news is NOT good news: it hurts.* And the pain continues to gnaw without some kind of closure, trust me on this. So I've had little choice but to eventually write farewell letters to those people who have not had the consideration to write back in *years*. It's particularly sad, but I've let go and can now move on.

The good news is that I join a growing number of transgender people who can report that a significant percentage of relationships have gotten *closer* for knowing the real person they've always been inside. Sharing such a personal truth can and should be seen as a TG's gesture of trust, respect, courage and the value of your relationship. If you are coping with such a transgender friend or relative, please take this to heart and *have* a little heart: some minimal human courtesy goes a long way.

## Co-workers

More and more transgender people are coming out as time goes on. There are lots of reasons for this, but a very big one is that they are a little more likely to *keep their jobs* after doing so. Next to family, the career is probably the most important issue to any TG considering transition to a new social identity. It's literally a matter of survival.

The encouraging news is that more TGs are keeping their jobs because a number of transgender advocacy organizations[31] have been working hard for many years with employers and government agencies to educate and pave the way for successful on-the-job transitions.

There is good reason aplenty for employers to retain productive employees who have announced that they are transgender. A company invests time and assets in training for positions at all levels, so it makes good business sense to reap the long-term rewards from that investment—and having been an employer myself for 25 years I can personally underscore this fact. Everyone knows that *there's no substitute for experience, so it's worth making a special effort to hang on to anyone who has it.*

At the risk of dredging up a rather hackneyed corporate cliché, a company really is a team—a team that is comprised of *people*, not just workers. And these people not only need to do a good job, they need to get along with one another. In these modern civilized times (*at least theoretically*), morale and productivity are indeed related. And who wants to spend 8+ hours a day being unhappy? So it is for the good of the company and the employees who spend their daily lives there that *everyone* get through a transgender on-the-job transition experience and into a productive long-term environment.

**Initial reactions to the news.** If you've recently learned that one of your co-workers is going to transition on the job, it's likely that this won't hit you at first as particularly joyful news. Getting your work done is tough enough, so who needs an issue like this to deal with on top of everything else, right? Let me offer a couple of thoughts in answer to that understandable question.

First of all, any announcement that involves a complete unknown is not going to be regarded as good news, no matter what the flavor of the underlying issue. What if the announcement were simply, "Good afternoon, ladies and gentlemen. This is to announce that there will be a change tomorrow. That is all." Responses are most likely to be variations on wary suspicion.

So it's no surprise that when it is announced that so-and-so is "transgender" and is going to transition on the job to the "opposite sex," your knee-jerk reaction could be something like, "You've got to be *kidding* me!"—with an accompanying roll of the eyeballs. It's a huge question mark, and a very controversial one at that.

If it's announced that someone is getting married, you *know* what that means and will react positively to this news (*unless you have some contradicting inside information*). Likewise a pregnancy, a graduation, even a death: you can cope with these because you *know* the process. But changing *sex*?? Holy cow! The mind reels.

**Prepare yourself: it works.** So here are a few things to think about that might ease your mind a little toward your transgender co-worker and the on-the-job transition process that's on the agenda.

• **Empathy**. Try to rustle up some well-deserved empathy for this person. A transition at work is *hugely* challenging for this TG. He or she is probably nervous, more than a little scared, and is trying to cope with a change that touches every single part of life.

Even if this seems to you like a totally crazy thing to do (*like, oh, getting your eyeballs pierced*), TGs are embracing this challenge squarely because they *have* to, there is just no effective alternative. But they *are* human and this is very difficult. If you can imagine for a moment how truly daunting this process can feel, you can understand why some TGs tragically choose suicide as a much more palatable option to what you are about to witness your co-worker go through. There's got to be at least a flicker of empathy glowing inside you somewhere.

• **Respect**. Even if this whole "sex-change thing" seems way too much to get your head around, try to focus on the *underlying principle* that drives this very risky and courageous step. It is for no other reason than to be *real*, to live in integrity instead of living a lie—in the face of overwhelming resistance. You've got to at least respect that a little bit, even if you don't agree with the particulars.

• **It's not a "lifestyle choice."** It's more appropriate to think of a sex-role change as the treatment for a birth condition—which in a real sense it often is. Remember our discussion in *Brain Sex and Gender* in Part I. Try to imagine feeling early in life that you're in the wrong *body*, for crying out loud, and that people just tell you "you're crazy" and then try to psychologically or physically beat it out of you. *A transgender nature is not something you believe in or just want to do, it's something you* ***are***. Had that person been allowed to live true to self from childhood, you wouldn't be reeling from having the sex-role rug suddenly pulled out from under you.

• **Prepare to be impressed**. A lot of TGs spend *staggering* amounts of time, effort and money to be the best man or woman they know how to be. Many do this so well that, had you not known of their past, you'd never guess that they used to be another sex (please visit **www.LearnAboutTransgender.org** and watch some of the videos on the *Face to Face* page to get an idea). If you're thinking, "No way is John going to look like a woman!" or vice versa for Jane, don't be so sure. These pictures and videos will show you what's possible. More importantly, if this person doesn't "measure up" to the your standards of a "passable" man or woman, remember that a lot of folks are born with physical challenges of all kinds. They deserve respect and consideration, especially since they have been burdened with extra difficulties that put a lot of strain on human character. Again, put yourself in this situation: how would *you* cope with a need this strong?

• **Show some tolerance: it's not that hard.** In some cases a co-worker will transition to a gender-variant or queer identity that does not fall into either sex-role that you are familiar with. This is where tolerance of human diversity of all kinds comes in. It is very critical that we as humans truly understand and embrace the valuable concept of *consideration*, the root of tolerance: it works both ways. People from other geographical cultures look a lot different than what you're familiar with, too. But in the end, past the visual trappings, *we're all just people trying to do our best* with the cards we've been dealt. Try not to let gender-blending blind you from the personality in front of you. You may or may not eventually enjoy spending that much time with this person, just like a lot of other individuals in the company. But you might at least try to get past the cover and read a few pages of the book.

• **This actually may not be the first for you.** If your reaction is, "Geez, I've never met a transgender person before," don't be so sure of *that*, either. These days it is more and more likely that you've seen or even met a transgender person but didn't know it at the time (*yes, play eerie déjà vu music here*). Knowing that so many trans men and women have integrated invisibly into society will take some of the assumed exotic strangeness out of this experience for you.

• **The bathroom is just no big deal.** Try to relax and think through the inevitable *bathroom* issue (why this is always such a huge problem continues to confound me). Changing sex doesn't automatically turn someone into a peeping Tom (or Tammie). This person is very motivated to respect the privacy and the "territory" that is claimed by either bathroom option. Some people think that the very act of changing a sex-role is an invasion of the rights of their sex; this view is frankly prejudiced and unreasonable.

Transgender people have *tremendous* respect for their target sex and gender, otherwise why would they risk everything to change into it? In fact, I will go on record as saying that a trans man or woman appreciates and cherishes his/her sex-role *much* more than most natal males or females. Think about *that*. Appreciation beats entitlement any day in my book. And if this person is gender queer, the real issues are *respect* and *discretion*, not "men" or "women" on the door; let the TG use the bathroom of choice and require that, like anyone else, he or she be respectful of privacy. End of story.

- **Give it time.** Changes in mannerisms, voice and the like might seem "fake" at first, because: a) they are different—you're still thinking of this person in the old role—and b) new mannerisms may be a little clumsy initially. Believe me, it's not easy to *unlearn* a lifetime of walking, talking and acting in another sex-role. Give him or her a chance to get good at it: they want this very badly and will work very hard, but it takes time.

- **Be positive: it's a simple and very doable *choice*.** Post-transition people now have the potential to be much happier people—so for them, at least, this is very good news. Be happy for them. Co-workers who feel better about themselves and life will very likely be much more pleasant to be around. *We each have the ability to be positive: it's just a matter of **choice**.*

- **Don't jump the gun.** Finally, try not to get too far ahead of the game. If you can be patient and get through a challenging and perhaps occasionally clumsy period of change, you're very likely to be pleasantly surprised at how well this person does in the new role.

So with the above pep talk ringing in your ears, let's go over some of the fundamentals of an on-the-job transition process.

**The Real Life Test**. A striking *visual* transformation often represents the biggest challenge for co-workers to get beyond. After all, we're dealing with the most observable category of our society: our sex-role.

In order for transitioning TGs to qualify for major surgeries, they must go through what is called the *Real Life Test* (RLT), more recently termed the *Real Life Experience* (RLE).[32] This requires them to live in their new sex-role full time, 24/7, for at least one year prior to obtaining the authorization for genital reassignment or other irreversible surgeries. This is a very difficult time for the TG, as he or she feels in a kind of limbo—living day to day while feeling incomplete. And it is often a challenging learning process—as well as a more difficult *un*learning one—for this person, so "cutting a little slack" is a very humane thing for co-workers to do.

**It's not just "looking the part," it's matching the inside.** If a trans woman (male to female) decides on Facial Feminization Surgery (FFS), this step can result in a significant and relatively immediate visual change. This surgery often involves substantial facial bone restructuring, requiring a recovery period of several weeks. The good news is that FFS can also be very effective in helping co-workers accept a trans woman in her new role.

FFS is not that well known for its significance in a transition because most people are too busy obsessing on the vastly over-emphasized genital reassignment issue (GRS), the results of which are not publicly visible (even in the bathroom—unless *you're* the peeping one). In contrast, FFS deals directly with a TG's social identity, serving a powerful role in a public transition.

Female to Male (FTM) transitions don't usually involve quite as dramatic a visual change in such a relatively short time frame. Most trans men will start receiving testosterone hormone therapy (or likely have started it before any announcement), the most significant results of which will be the gradual appearance of facial hair, lowering of voice pitch, increased body hair and the like. The most immediate visual changes for a trans man might be hair and clothing style, followed by the oft-undergone chest surgery. Since most trans men bind their breasts early on if these are substantial (by wrapping them tightly with elastic banding), the results of breast reduction surgery may not be that dramatic at work.

**Different appearance, same or better performance.** At no time during this challenging on-the-job transition period should there be any unreasonable assumptions about this employee's ability to do the job just because he or she has an open transgender issue to deal with. It is almost always the case that he or she has been dealing with it for years already: transition is actually a step toward *resolution* and the ability to be a better person.

▼ **In a tolerant environment, transgender employees are very likely to become more productive after transition, because they've alleviated the significant stress and energy drain of not being able to live and work as their real selves.**

It's likely that the early stages of transition on the job will be somewhat distracting to those directly involved. Then again *so can a pregnancy, a heart operation, and other significant life events.* Everyone wants the TG's new role to be a non-issue, especially the TG. As far as the work goes, all that transgender employees ask for is a fair chance, and they deserve it. They just want everyone to relax and let them do a good job. ***TGs want to be known and appreciated for who they ARE, not "what" they are or who they were.***

## Changes, Threats and Opportunities

If we'd all grown up with our real human diversity understood and allowed by family and society, we wouldn't find ourselves in the tough pickle of having someone jump the sex-role tracks out of nowhere and give us all brain hemorrhages trying to rethink the whole thing. It's a difficult situation for everyone involved, but it's one that can be virtually eliminated in the future through *education* and a widespread understanding of the *actual diversity of human sexuality*.

Dealing with a transgender identity is but one of countless challenging situations where we find ourselves coping with significant *change* in our lives: in a relationship, a perspective, a new knowledge, a belief system, or all of the above.

**Change is the only constant in this life.** It's true that change can be unsettling, even threatening: we want security in our lives and the very thought of change seems to put it at risk. A 6-year-old once told me, "I *hate* change because everything is *different!*" From the mouths of babes . . . But change is, in a complex, sapient and adaptive species like human beings, both inevitable and constant.

It is important to remember, especially in transgender transitions, that:

⚧ **Change has as much of a chance of being an opportunity for growth as it does being a threat to our security.**

If you really think about it, true security in this life is a tenuous thing, probably a lot more imagined by fearful minds than real.

Would it not be wiser to face up to how insecure life really is, and to learn how to successfully cope with this fact? Hiding behind a false sense of security sets us up to panic when we think it is threatened, instead of fostering the confidence that we possess the ability to survive successfully because we're capable of it.

Avoiding change is, in a sense, delaying the inevitable in so many facets of life. As we as humans grow in knowledge through research, analyses and introspection, responding to a myriad of discoveries is more a matter of *when* than *if.*

**Traditions** do have social and familial value, but these can survive and even embrace change by incorporating it into the tradition—or even creating new ones. Traditions can also provide a source of stability that gives us strength and perspective to cope with inevitable change all around us. But it's important to realize this:

❦ **To use traditions or traditional thinking to shield against new truths and the changes that these are bound to precipitate is seldom wise, especially in the long run.**

**We most often find only what we're looking for.** It is also true that as individuals we are most likely to find only those things we're actually looking for in this life. So if we expect that changes are inherently threats then it is quite likely that we'll fulfill our own prophecy.

Conversely *if we encounter something—or someone—that seems to threaten our belief system, understanding this as an opportunity to learn and even become more adept in our beliefs can be much to our eventual benefit.* Hiding from change is seldom a viable long term solution (*chameleons notwithstanding*).

As we discussed earlier in Part III, feelings like the fear of change are best examined as objectively as possible before making any decisions as to how to respond to them. Looking for *opportunity* rather than threat in situations of change will enable us to benefit from growth. Being *open* to opportunity is an attitude that has huge potential for good in our lives; there is virtually nothing to lose by staying open, and moreover everything to potentially gain by it.

**Threat or opportunity?** A transgender life-change may *feel* unsettling and even threatening to you, your relationship or your belief system. But it's important to remember that feelings are motivators to *explore their roots and to work through them*, not to react without sufficient thought. Stop and ask yourself frankly, "Why exactly does this bother me?" Peel away the layers of feelings and rationale until you get to the core: perhaps you are afraid of something in yourself, and that's a good thing to understand because *you can now deal with it.* None of us can address and solve any problem until we know exactly what it is.

Another word for reacting to fear without thought is *panic*, and as a pilot with over 35 years' experience who's still alive through all manner of airborne emergencies I can tell you firsthand that panic is the last thing you ever want to do in a situation of threat. (*"I'll wet my pants later; right now I'm too busy getting this aircraft down in one piece."*)

Deciding how to respond to a transgender transition is not something you have to do in a matter of seconds, thank heavens. ***Give yourself time to absorb all the ramifications***, to learn something new, to explore, to evaluate, to talk with others, to see the possibility of incorporating this perspective into your world-view and having one less unknown that you fear simply because it *is* an unknown. In the end you retain the choice whether or not to be involved personally with a TG in your life, but it's a *well-informed* choice.

⚧ **We human beings have thrived on this planet not because we're all that strong or big or quick, but because we can LEARN.**

While it is true that fear produces the animal urge for fight or flight, our real secret weapon for survival and coping is our intelligence and capability for reasoning and *learning*. Keeping this in mind while dealing with transgender issues will be greatly to your own benefit.

As to how we discern a threat to us, disagreement in perspective or practice is not grounds for immediate defensiveness and intolerance if that difference does not *objectively* and *actually* harm anyone.

▽ **Feeling threatened is not necessarily the same as actually *being* threatened.**

This is an important distinction that lies at the root of all manner of discrimination and hate crimes in this world. Every perceived threat needs to be worked through rationally and fairly, likely involving compromises, tolerance, and many shades of grey. As much as people would prefer a tidy world of black and white, life on this planet comes in many colors, and the colors are changing all the time. Most biologists will tell you that one long-standing law of nature is "adapt or die out." A bit harsh, but it indicates the life-saving value of *flexibility*. It is something that we can apply to a social environment as well.

In the end I believe it is very helpful for us to know this:

▽ **We have much more *choice* in how we approach all things in life than we usually realize at any given time.**

Reacting in fear often blinds us to the fact that we *do* have choices in how to respond to most any situation. In fact, ***being happy is in itself something we must choose to do at every opportunity***. A good word for deciding thusly is *attitude*: a positive attitude in life is recognizing that we *do* have a choice, and that we can *choose* to pursue happiness. Sadly I have observed that many people work very hard at being *un*happy: they unwittingly are choosing to be so at virtually every opportunity.

*Every one of us has a choice in how we respond to a transgender person in our lives.* We can choose to panic, to run away in fear, to stubbornly reject or ostracize, to consider, to learn, to benefit or to grow from this experience. It is a very rare situation indeed where we truly have no choice; and *considering* the perspective of a transgender person in our lives is not one of those situations.

**Change, growth and inspiration.** There is a certain kind of change that is very important for pretty much all life on this earth: *growth*. When a transgender person makes such a profound life-change, it is appropriate to see this as a kind of significant step toward self-actualization, fulfillment, integrity, and greater happiness—no guarantees, mind you, but *it is a step that opens up opportunities*.

I have observed, sadly, that people can actually react negatively to other people's growth and improvement, feeling envious and fearfully defensive about it. For example, if a member of a street gang decides to go back to school and pursue a better life, this can be cause for serious derision from the rest of the gang. This is a defensive response in order to "save face" for all those who don't have the drive to better themselves. Personal growth can, in this respect, be a "threat" to the fragile egos of others.

On the other hand, witnessing a transgender transition can also be a powerful inspiration: that people really *can* change their lives, and dramatically so, if they want to badly enough. That's something for us all to think about, whether we're stuck in a dead-end job, a bad relationship, battling weight problems, in a depressing rut: wherever we are struggling with the need to make changes in our lives.

Yes: we do have a choice in just about everything we face. How will *you* choose to regard the transgender people in your life?

# Human Diversity, Human Rights

Throughout this book I've bandied about the terms "human rights" and "civil rights," in this case with respect to various aspects of sexual and gender diversity. It's easy to take these terms at face value, assuming we all think the same things in response to such concepts. Yet the *specific* fundamentals of "human rights" are shockingly seldom talked about in our day-to-day lives, from the political arena down to the dinner table.

So I think it's appropriate to spend a few final moments to confirm the universal nature of many of the challenges and issues we encountered in the more specific situations of relating to diverse sexualities.

One of the greatest challenges that transgender people face, beyond the many relational ones we talked about, is that of claiming the few fundamental human rights to which a majority of the population feels every human being is entitled—at least according to many official proclamations that we'll cover shortly. So let's examine more closely some of the more relevant universal rights that affect all manner of diverse people.

**Human rights go gold.** Most would agree that the earliest written statements of the more universal human social ethics were through religious expression, as early as the ancient Indian, Babylonian and Egyptian empires. To this day there is one common theme that runs through almost every religious faith, which has in relatively modern times taken the title of the "Golden Rule" or "Ethic of Reciprocity."

The Parliament of the World's Religions proclaimed the Golden

Rule as the common principle for many religions in its *"Declaration Toward a Global Ethic"* in 1993.[33] This ethic has been expressed in both positive and negative forms ("treat" or "don't treat" others) but essentially means the same thing:

⚧ **The Golden Rule** in its positive and negative forms:
Positive: **Treat others as you would want to be treated.**
Negative: **Do not treat others in ways you would not want to be treated** (sometimes called the "Silver Rule").[34]

The commonality of the Golden Rule across so many religious faiths is probably because it is a ***sociological*** ethic rather than a theological construct. It points out how humans must treat *one another* in order to succeed as a social species; it is independent of the involvement of specific deities. But it does require that we recognize such things as good and harmful (or constructive and destructive). Whether these two classes of human behavior fall into the sociological or spiritual realm is a matter of perspective that doesn't change the influence of these on the whole of humanity.

We could also think of the Golden Rule as a broader definition of being *humane*, as we discussed earlier. Yet it is also more than just an ideal for which we strive, it is also fundamentally *practical* in its application to social beings:

⚧ **The Golden Rule is actually a very *practical* rule for a social species like humans, for if we do this simple thing (entirely possible for everyone to do) then equality, social justice and the right to human fulfillment are accessible to *all* people.**

To our great misfortune, however, history has shown that the human race has been abysmally poor in executing this simple Golden Rule; all too often what is actually executed is: *people*.

So the most basic individual and social freedoms promised

by any democracy are ultimately impossible without the Golden Rule remaining *universal*. As idealistic as the rule might seem, it is actually where the rubber meets the road of day-to-day life.

▽ **Whether we're talking about a partner, family, friends, neighborhood, school, work, government, or international relations, the Golden Rule is the critical foundation for providing every individual equal access to the pursuit of human fulfillment without harm.**

So why can't we do this simple thing, to at least "live and let live" as this rule has been colloquially expressed? One answer: *it is in the process of applying a universal ethic to the dynamic, organic, and extremely complex interactions between essentially flawed human beings that things get challenging to the extreme.* Especially when a significant segment of any population just plain refuses to cooperate and intentionally tries to beat the system through distortion, obfuscation, exploitation, manipulation or anything else that does the selfish job for them.

**Hypocrisy.** The term for directly—and most often knowingly—violating the Golden Rule is *hypocrisy*, and it is a most destructive human capacity that fuels individual/corporate/political exploitation, suppression, invasive conquest, tyranny, barbarism, torture and genocide (*none of which looks very good on a resumé*). Of grave concern, of course, is the fact that the steady progress of weapons and control technologies—from the Stone Age to financial/informational manipulation to nuclear weapons—has rendered hypocrisy more and more lethal over the centuries. *So the presence of even a little hypocrisy is extremely dangerous because even a few humans are capable of affecting innocent people by the millions*, as we unfortunately observe every day around the globe.

And hypocrisy lies at the root of a principle topic of this book: *sexism. People are treated in ways they don't want to be treated, simply because of the sex they are born into, by people who would surely not wish to be treated thusly.*

So even though we humans are inherently quite capable of interpreting the elegantly simple universal Golden Rule, the persistent presence of hypocrisy in most every population forces us to literally spell it out: one condition at a time, again and again.

**Modern human rights declarations.** Secular forerunners of the modern concept of human rights have existed in many forms throughout recorded history, with limited and somewhat political versions declared in the ancient Greek and Roman empires—although slavery was widely and deplorably justified as a "natural condition" until the 19th century.

*The Twelve Articles*, developed in Europe in 1525 in response to the German Peasant's War, are considered by many to be the first modern written statement of universal human rights. In 1683 the *English Bill of Rights* and Scottish *Claim of Right* were written to address a number of oppressive governmental policies. In the 18th century both the American and French Revolutions took place, leading to the American *Declaration of Independence* and the French *Declaration of the Rights of Man and of the Citizen*.[34]

This first formal American national document includes a core statement of human rights at the beginning of the second paragraph: *"We hold these truths to be self-evident, that all men [humans] are created equal, that they are endowed by their Creator with certain unalienable rights, that among these are life, liberty and the pursuit of happiness."*

This eloquent expression of human rights is readily acceptable by any reasonable person. Yet so many obvious applications of this ethic—such as the abolition of slavery and women's suffrage that now, looking back, are embarrassingly straightforward—have been met with stubborn and formidable resistance that continues to this day. Case in point: in spite of widespread honest personal testimony and mounting scientific evidence to the contrary, an alarming number of people cling to the erroneous belief that sexual orientation and gender identity are lifestyle *choices*. To insist that people would *choose* widespread discrimination fails not only fact but rationality as well.

So the process of spelling out what *should* be clear to anyone of conscience has been a painfully long and laborious process, as is evidenced by the history of the *United States Constitution*, for one.

The Constitution, in its original form adopted in 1787, chiefly outlined the structural and procedural system of the federal government and limitations of states. It wasn't until four years later that the first ten Amendments were adopted and collectively referred to as the *Bill of Rights*. These amendments, as the title suggests, focused more on the fundamental human rights that our nation's early lawmakers felt needed to be included specifically. Since then there have been seventeen more amendments, including those addressing human rights, spanning more than two hundred years.

The following Constitutional Amendments deal with the more universal human rights:
- 1st Amendment: freedom of expression, religion, and press;
- 13th Amendment: slavery is abolished;
- 15th Amendment: men of all races allowed to vote;
- 19th Amendment: women's right to vote.

Many of the human rights articulated by the Declaration of Independence and the current U.S. Constitution are elaborated *internationally* in the current United Nations covenants, so let's explore these briefly as they pertain to transgender people.

**United Nations Human Rights Covenants.** The atrocities of World Wars I and II galvanized modern international efforts to define, propagate and eventually ensure a set of human rights, to at least turn the tide against such massive destruction if not pave the way for progress toward global and individual peace and prosperity.

The United Nations General Assembly adopted the first *Universal Declaration of Human Rights* in 1948, framed by the UN Human Rights Commission (now the UN Human Rights Council). Because of considerable debate over the nature of civil/political rights versus economic/social/cultural ones, the Commission eventually split the declaration into two sets of covenants:

**The International Covenant on Civil and Political Rights**—abbreviated **ICCPR**, and

**The International Covenant on Economic, Social and Cultural Rights**—abbreviated **ICESCR**.

These two covenants cross-reference one another by sharing the same initial article:

*Part I, Article 1.1: All peoples have the right of self-determination. By virtue of that right they freely determine their political status and freely pursue their economic, social and cultural development.*[35]

The ICCPR then continues on with civil/political issues such as legal remedy for violations, physical safety, right-to-life, prohibition of torture, security of person, procedural fairness, liberty in movement, right to vote and so forth.

The ICESCR, which focuses on economic, cultural and social rights, contains the following articles that are most appropriate for the diversity issues in this book:

*Part III, Article 19.1: Everyone shall have the right to hold opinions without interference.*

*Part III, Article 19.2: Everyone shall have the right to freedom of expression; this right shall include freedom to seek, receive and impart information and ideas of all kinds, regardless of frontiers, either orally, in writing or in print, in the form of art, or through any other media of his choice.*[36]

Essentially these articles, along with several others, spell out more specifically the rights to "life, liberty and the pursuit of happiness," which the UN Preamble states "derive from the inherent dignity of the human person." These three articles are, in my opinion, the most fundamentally relevant to the topic of this book.

**Applying the UN Human Rights Articles to diverse sexualities.** Having recognized just these three articles of human rights, let's now take the next step and apply these to people with diverse sexualities through more specific language:

*1. Transgender people have the right to determine their own sexual and gender identities (the right to self-determination).*
*2. Transgender people have the right to embrace this identity without interference (the right to hold their opinion on their own identities).*
*3. Transgender people have the right to express their identities, through personality, mannerisms, dress and so forth, without interference, discrimination, suppression or harm (right to freedom of expression).*

Regardless of any personal discomfort with diverse sexualities, or an incompatibility with one's religious faith or personal preferences, one can't argue that the above fundamental rights lie well within the United Nations human rights covenants. Importantly, ***they do not detract in any way from any of the same rights of other human beings***, even though many people may *feel* threatened by them. So it should be impossible to justify any form of discrimination—socially, legally or otherwise—on people with diverse identities: in the family, the community, the workplace or the government.

**The things we allow.** The gross violations of human rights, of the degree that motivated the UN Covenants, are of course significantly enabled by ever-developing technologies and their perverted potential for destruction. Similarly the accumulation of significant wealth enables powerful control and exploitation of so many by so few.

And yet another more subtle factor plays an important role in the acquisition of control, and it is this: *the ultimate power to oppress a population is often assembled incrementally over time because the majority of us **allow** it to happen, step by step.* A few people mesmerize, misinform and manipulate populations into essentially handing over control largely willingly.

It often starts with a relatively small faction, gains momentum steadily, and in a few years Hitler or Stalin or Pol Pot have acquired massive control: not single-handedly, but through the awesome power that so many citizens *gave* to them over time. A few dominators can't do it alone: it requires a lot of personal loyalty and obedience, from individual military personnel on down. All of this launched from a platform of discriminating against a target group: be it for ethnicity, race, religion, class, ideology or sexual diversity. Which is why it is so critical to identify and eliminate all discrimination *at the onset*.

**Defending the Golden Rule.** People like Ghandi gave us a great model for protecting the Golden Rule against oppression, often termed "non-violent resistance or "peaceful civil disobedience." It's a very humane response to the specific efforts of dominators: by simply refusing their unjust demands *en masse*. The challenge, of course, is actually mobilizing the reluctant into a *masse* large enough to challenge an oppressive authority, but it does happen. In these cases the disobedience refers actually to the resistance against the oppressive directives of these dominators. ***So in a real sense it is not actually disobedience, it is rather obedience to a higher authority: the Golden Rule.***

Which is why it is so critical to keep this fundamental ethic front-of-mind in everything we do, large and small, at work or school or at home or in government office. Until we can steadfastly and actively adhere to this most fundamental ethic of human rights, the pendulum of domination will continue to swing ever farther, its increasing perturbations fueled by manipulative and destructive technologies and wealth, until the unthinkable happens.

Can we prevent this? The trends of the nightly news are not encouraging. Yet I, for one, believe in my heart that human beings are for the most part *humane* beings, that we have in us the capability for so much good on this earth. But as the saying goes, "evil triumphs when good people do nothing."

▽ **It is our collective failure to stay true to the most basic humane ethics, down to the small day-to-day things, that eventually empowers the few to dominate and exploit the many to their selfish end.**

We must ask ourselves in all things, large and small, "What am I allowing to happen *today* that I shouldn't?" And then, importantly, take peaceful *action* to rectify it, one small step at a time.

There is an excellent expression of the dangers of allowing the loss of *any* freedoms, attributed to German Pastor Martin Niemöller, describing his disappointment at the local intellectuals' response to the Nazi party's purging of chosen peoples. Though it is stated in many forms, specifying different groups, here is one version:

*First they came for the socialists,*
*and I did not speak out because I was not a socialist.*
*Then they came for the trade unionists,*
*and I did not speak out because I was not a trade unionist.*
*Then they came for the Jews,*
*and I did not speak out because I was not a Jew.*
*Then they came for me*
*And there was no one left to speak for me.*[37]

I'm careful to add here that the Nazi party was not an outgrowth of German ethnicity, it was the product of a small group of dominators that just happened in this case to be German. Unfortunately these particular tyrants, whose actions have been so well documented, have a lot of company from virtually every nationality and ethnicity across the globe and throughout history.

So the above observations, applied to the topic of this book, amount to this:

▼ **If we stand by and allow harmless transgender people to be discriminated against, legislated against, ostracized by society, banned from the workplace and even killed through hate crimes, this very permission can eventually lead to our own loss of the fundamental freedoms to which we are all entitled.**

We must stand for each others' human rights—*especially if we don't agree with the particulars*—if we have any hope of maintaining our own freedoms. We *can* do this; the question is: will enough of us do so, soon enough?

**Embracing our ability to re-focus.** Working toward real social justice involves sorting through a tangle of personal preferences, traditional thinking, religious perspectives and social prejudice, which is daunting to be sure—and it will take time and deliberation as outlined in this section.

Yet when you get right down to it, ***our energy tends to go where we focus it***. So it would be most constructive for all of us to consider this fact every single day:

▼ **If we realize that we *can* re-direct our focus from obsessing on our differences to embracing our inherent human capacity for mutual support and compassion, then we can actually make considerable progress towards peaceful coexistence.**

Most of us share the goal of pursuing personal happiness without harm. Yet we too often get blinded by myopically concentrating on dogmatic, ethnic or sexual differences instead of focusing on our *many* commonalities and our significant capability for cooperation and synergy. In fact our capacity for coming together in spite of differences is revealed now and then on a large scale:

**☢ Time and again our compassionate responses to disasters prove our human capability to come together in support, regardless of the many differences we otherwise inflate out of proportion.**

Sadly it takes a dire situation of some kind to wake people up to the fact that we *can* come together through empathy and do great things *for* and *with* one another. It demonstrates graphically that we are perfectly capable of this—and as the Golden Rule promises *everyone* benefits by it, not just a few.

**Why honor human rights?** Time and again it has been proven that humans are inherently capable of tolerance, cooperation, compassion and yes, even love. And to put it bluntly, I believe this:

**☢ It is precisely because we ARE capable of *humane* qualities that we are ethically bound to embrace them.**

To refuse to do so is in a very real sense a perversion of our nature, a destructive failure to attain our naturally-endowed potential.

I believe that humans possess an essential capacity for *conscience*, as an intelligent extension of the degree of consciousness to which we have evolved—or been endowed, depending on your perspective. In any case it comes to this:

**☢ Our inherent human capacity for *conscience* is what binds us to human rights and the Golden Rule.**

Although conscience is often defined as "a knowledge or sense of right and wrong, with an urge to do right,"[38] the concepts of "right" and "wrong" are subject to personal interpretation. So I see the meaning of "conscience" in perhaps more fundamental terms, as suggested from the root word *conscire*: < *con-*, with + *scire*, to know. In other words, *with an ability to discern (the truth)*.

▼ **Conscience could be essentially defined as our ability to perceive the constructive good or the destructive harm we cause to others as a result of our individual actions or inactions.**

In other words, *to recognize the truthful consequences of our personal involvement in the real world around us*.

Unfortunately this endowment is all too frequently negated by our flawed human ability to *ignore our own conscience*. We are too often ruled by our internal "kings and queens of *denial*." Such widespread denial is a nearly impregnable force that empowers hypocrisy. It is ***willful ignorance***, a tragic human failure to uphold our natural capability.

**Ultimately it's personal.** Inasmuch as we are so stubbornly embroiled in discrimination and suppression over *beliefs* and *issues*, it is important to cut through it all to realize that ultimately it's *personal*. For in fact **anything that involves people is personal**, there's no way around that. To repeatedly dehumanize people into such things as "consumers" or "nationalities" or "denominations" paves the way for all manner of discrimination, exploitation, domination and even eradication.

Far too many times I've heard the phrase, "This isn't personal, it's business." This false dichotomy merely creates an "acceptable" excuse for the financial exploitation of *people*. ***Wise businesspeople know that in the end business is really all about*** **relationships**. And I can personally attest to this with 35 years of business experience, including international commerce.

With regard to the specific issues addressed in this book, people often continue to find many transgender issues difficult to consider—until it finally takes on a *personal* element (which is why I've woven just a few of my own experiences into this book). Once we see firsthand someone who is another living breathing human being, struggling and trying to do the right thing in the face of widespread adversity, we can now experience empathy and even compassion. *This kind of human consciousness is a key factor in being able to finally consider perspectives that we remained closed to without experiencing the personal nature of these issues.*

For the fact is that **relationships are critical to our well-being**, as anyone experiencing solitary confinement would attest (*and Daniel Defoe told well*). Although knowledge and achievement are valuable and rewarding, it is also true that:

⚧ **Mutually constructive personal interaction is a critical source of real human fulfillment.**

And this is because the greatest human attribute that has been bestowed upon us—one that we should never forget for a moment in all things—is our capacity for *love*.

**The human need for love: of self and others.** If there is any credibility to eons of literature, religion, art and music, we humans possess an inherent need to love and be loved. For this we need *each other*—loved ones, friends and community—to be truly fulfilled, humanly happy.

We need to *share* joys and sadness, support and stress, achievements and frustrations to really get fulfillment from them or to be able to just carry on. If we focus exclusively on our own needs and perspectives, we will eventually lose the friends and loved ones that we so essentially need for our own happiness and even survival.

Transgender people desire to live honestly with the people around them that they need for the fundamental human fulfillment they seek. Only in so doing can they love and be loved ***truly***, something we *all* yearn for to our very core.

The catch for transgender people, however, is the *true selves* part. ***It is difficult, if not impossible, to love others if you don't know and therefore love yourself.*** If one's Core Identity has been buried out of sight by society and family, it's impossible to know and love your true self, and therefore be able to truly love others.

☿ **Only in knowing our true selves, and accepting and loving that self "warts and all," can we be empowered to truly love and be loved.**

This is not an easy truth for an inherently flawed human race to actually embrace (*especially the part about the warts*). For transgender people this is particularly difficult since society is telling them at every turn that they are fundamentally wrong and essentially unlovable to anyone much less themselves (*the message being that transgender people **are** warts*).

For those transgender folks who are lucky enough to finally discover and actually embrace their true selves, ***the cathartic realization of the newfound opportunity to truly love and be loved is one of the most powerful life experiences imaginable.*** I will *never* forget the exact moment that this happened for me.

And it is this true love of self that enables a most precious human quality: graciousness. *For it is **human grace** that binds consideration, empathy, compassion and human imperfection together into the greatest gift of all: love.*

**There is no substitute for love.** Think very hard about this. In spite of the staggering efforts of so many people over the centuries to acquire wealth and control, to dominate, discriminate and even eradicate, these are so often tragically misguided substitutes for the one thing we need the most as humans: to simply love as, and be loved for, who we truly are.

**▽ There are indeed many other worthy and exceedingly valuable goals in this life, but none of these can take the place of the critical human need to love and be loved.**

And moreover, *we simply cannot deny people this fundamental human need just because they are harmlessly different than we are.*

I propose that Leo Buscaglia's powerful book *Love: A Warm and Wonderful Book About the Largest Experience In Life* be required reading in every beginning high school curriculum around the world.[39] I encourage *you* to read this book as soon as possible if you haven't. (It is currently out of print but copies can be found via the internet and used book stores, very much worth the search.)

In the end, transgender people ask only to be allowed to embrace and live out their core identities, without harm. William Shakespeare knew well the ultimate value of this critical ethic in the whole scheme of life. He wrote in *Hamlet*, Act I, Scene III:

**"This above all: to thine own self be true."**

The opportunity to be true to themselves, and thus to truly love and be loved, is all that transgender people ask of our society. Can we not give each other this simple right?

▽

# Notes and References

1. *Webster's New World College Dictionary*, Wiley Publishing, 2007, p. 580 gives the following lengthy definitions of gender: "1. Gram. a) the formal classification by which nouns are grouped and inflected, or changed in form, so as to reflect certain syntactic relationships: pronouns, modifiers, and verbs may also be so inflected; although gender is not a formal feature of English, some nouns and the third person singular pronouns are distinguished according to sex or the lack of sex (Ex.: *man* or *he*, masculine gender; *woman* or *she*, feminine gender; *door* or *it*, neuter gender): in most Indo-European languages, as well as in many others, gender is not necessarily correlated with sex. b) any one of such groupings, or an inflectional form showing membership in such a group 2. the fact or condition of being a male or a female human being, esp. with regard to how this affects or determines a person's self-image, social status, goals, etc." (*Note: the vagueness of the above is one reason why we must specify a meaning for gender and distinguish it from the word sex for which it is widely confused. - Ed.*) Other definitions stated as being from Webster are taken from this publication.

2. Brown & Rounsley, *True Selves*, (Josey-Bass, 1996), p. 19.

3. The dismantling of the sexually determinative construct began with such studies as those of Dr. Alfred Kinsey (Kinsey, A., Pomeroy, W., & Martin, C. *Sexual Behavior in the Human Male*, 1948, Philadelphia: Saunders; Kinsey, A., Pomeroy, W., Martin, C., & Gebhard, R. *Sexual Behavior in the Human Female*, 1953, Philadelphia: Saunders), and continued with many publications such as the eventual removal of homosexuality as a diagnostic disorder in the *Diagnostic Statistical Manual of Psychiatry* beginning in 1973 (see the section in this book

entitled "Whose disorder is it, anyway?" beginning on p. 69 for more detail), medical studies on the diversity of brain structure in males and females (see the section on "Brain sex and gender" beginning on p. 42 for further references) and copious gender studies literature such as Bullough and Bullough *Crossdressing, Gender and Sex*, 1993, University of Pennsylvania Press), Brown & Rounsley's *True Selves* (Josey-Bass, 1996), Fausto-Sterling's *Sexing the Body* (Basic Books, 2000), Roughgarden's *Evolution's Rainbow* (University of California Press, 2004), Arlene Lev's comprehensive *Transgender Emergence* (Hawthorne Press, 2004, e.g. p. 16), and many more.

4. Ann Fausto-Sterling *Sexing the Body*, Basic Books, 2000, p. 20; Julia Serano, *Whipping Girl*, Seal Press, 2007, p. 13; Lev, A. *Transgender Emergence*, Hawthorne Press, 2004, p. 80.

5. Gray, J. *Men Are From Mars, Women Are From Venus*, Harper Collins Publishers, 1992.

6. Lev, A. *Transgender Emergence*, Hawthorne Press, 2004, p. 57.

7. For examples of identical twin cases, refer to: 1) the documentary film *Red Without Blue*, that "follows a pair of identical twins as one transitions from male to female;" more information can be found at www.redwithoutblue.com; 2) ABC News Good Morning America release entitled *Transgender Twin Offers New Insight* found at http://abcnews.go.com/GMA/Health/Story?id=174855&page=1; and The Oprah Winfrey Show coverage entitled *Transgendered Twins*, found at www.oprah.com/slideshow/oprahshow/oprahshow1_ss_20050916. Segal, Nancy *Entwined Lives: Twins and What They Tell Us About Human Behavior*, Dutton Adult, 1999.

8. Lev, A. *Transgender Emergence*, Hawthorne Press, 2004, pp. 79-109; Fausto-Sterling, A., *Sexing the Body* (Basic Books, 2000), pp. 1-29; Serano, J. *Whipping Girl*, Seal Press, 2007, pp. 23-34, 77-93; Bornstein, K., *Gender Outlaw*, Vintage Books, 1994, pp. 21-40; Brown & Rounsley's *True Selves* (Josey-Bass, 1996), pp. 18-25; Roughgarden's *Evolution's Rainbow* (University of California Press, 2004), pp. 229-261.

9. Lev, A. *Transgender Emergence*, Hawthorne Press, 2004, p. 81.

10. Serano, J. *Whipping Girl*, Seal Press, 2007, p. 78; Lev, A. *Transgender Emergence*, Hawthorne Press, 2004, pp. 16, 80. *(Note: Serano uses the term "subconscious sex" to mean somewhat the same thing as Core Sexual Identity; likewise Lev describes a core sexual identity that is a combination of biological and identity factors. My use of the terms Core Gender Identity and Core Sexual Identity are offered as part of a simplified but nonetheless operational model of fundamental sexuality factors. I have provided these references not to suggest that these authors agree with my terms, but to rather give the reader resources to compare my terms with others in the field. Both of these authors influenced the development of my model or some aspects thereof, for which I am very grateful. –Ed.)*

11. Julia Serano, *Whipping Girl*, Seal Press, 2007, p. 33.

12. Moir & Jessel, *Brain Sex*, Dell, 1991, pp. 23-28, 38-49; *Netherlands Institute for Brain Research*, published in 1995 and 2000; Zhou, J. N., Hofman, M. A., Gooren, L. J., & Swaab, D. F. (1995); "A sex difference in the human brain and its relation to transsexuality," *Nature, 378*, pp. 68-70; Roughgarden, J., *Evolution's Rainbow*, Univ. of California Press, 2004, pp. 226-232; Fausto-Sterling, A., *Sexing the Body* (Basic Books, 2000), pp. 115-145; Lev, A. *Transgender Emergence*, Hawthorne Press, 2004, p. 119.

13. Roughgarden, J., *Evolution's Rainbow* (University of California Press, 2004), p. 230.

14. Roughgarden, J., *Evolution's Rainbow* (University of California Press, 2004), p. 240.

15. Moir & Jessel, *Brain Sex*, Dell, 1991, pp. 23-28.

16. Lev, A. *Transgender Emergence*, Hawthorne Press, 2004, pp. 81-83; Roughgarden, J., *Evolution's Rainbow* (University of California Press, 2004), pp. 241-242, 257.

17. Moir & Jessel, *Brain Sex*, Dell, 1991, p. 24.

18. Roughgarden, J., *Evolution's Rainbow* (University of California Press, 2004), pp. 242-244.

19. Lev, A. *Transgender Emergence*, Hawthorne Press, 2004, p. 116; Roughgarden, J., *Evolution's Rainbow* (University of California Press,

2004), p. 244.

20. Lev, A. *Transgender Emergence*, Hawthorne Press, 2004, p. 76.

21. Moir & Jessel, *Brain Sex*, Dell, 1991, pp. 23-28; Lev, A. *Transgender Emergence*, Hawthorne Press, 2004, pp. 81-83; Roughgarden, J., *Evolution's Rainbow* (University of California Press, 2004), pp. 241-244, 257.

22. Maslow, A., "A Theory of Human Motivation," *Psychological Review*, Vol. 50, No. 4, pp. 370-396.

23. American Psychiatric Association, *Diagnostic and Statistical Manual of Mental Disorders*, 2004, 302.6.

24. The diversity of the transgender population has somewhat worked against developing language that is consistent and specific. Transgender pioneer Virginia Prince coined the term "bigender" to describe those who spend part of their time in one gender role and part in another; this word distinguished itself from the term "cross-dresser" as being about gender behavior and not just clothes. The problem with this word, according to many TGs I've associated with over the years, is that it sounds too similar to "bisexual", suggesting that it is a sexual thing—and since people already confuse the terms sex and gender this is not surprising. In order to clear up some of the ambiguity the term "cogender" is offered to indicate that many trans people have two somewhat polar genders *co-existing* within themselves, and desire to express these by regularly spending time in each gender expression. The term "bigender" would be a better counterpart to "bisexual," both of these terms being an aspect of Relational Identity.

25. Ms. Bornstein gave two presentations at the Links and Alliances Conference at Everett Community College, Everett, WA on October 21, 2006. I was fortunate enough to attend this conference, hear Kate's presentations and to meet her (a real honor for me). These three conditions for good sex I've quoted to the best of my memory, since I was unable to take notes during this particular segment of her presentation.

26. Lev, A. *Transgender Emergence*, Hawthorne Press, 2004, p. 13.

27. American Psychiatric Association POSITION STATEMENT: *Therapies Focused on Attempts to Change Sexual Orientation (Reparative*

# Notes and References 165

*or Conversion Therapies),* Approved by the Board of Trustees, March 2000; on the web at http://www.critpath.org/pflag-talk/tgKIDfaq.html: "There is no known cure or course of treatment which reverses the transgender[ed] person's manifestation of the characteristics and behaviors of another gender. Transgender[ed] people have at times been subjected to electric shock therapy, aversion therapy (applying physical pain to condition response), drug therapy and other procedures. None of these 'cures' have succeeded."

28. Lev, A. *Transgender Emergence*, Hawthorne Press, 2004, p. 49. (Note: while this system was established for the protection of TGs against "inappropriate" medical decisions, it is regarded by some in the transgender community to be discriminatory compared to the relatively unrestricted access that non-trans people, that is "cissexuals," enjoy to elective plastic surgeries. This well-meaning form of "gatekeeper" authorization hinges on the inappropriate diagnosis of gender diversity as being a "disorder," which many believe in fact it is not (see the section *Responding to the Core* in Part II of this book). A complete presentation of the HBIGDA standards can be found on the web site www.wpath.org.

29. On the web at http://www.recover-from-grief.com/7-stages-of-grief.html, 2009. (*I have edited the text slightly as noted to make this model more appropriate for a transgender situation, with my sincere thanks and credit to the hosts of this site. -Ed.*)

30. Brill S. & Pepper R., *The Transgender Child*, Cleis Press, 2008.

31. Please visit the web site http://www.LearnAboutTransgender.org for a complete list of these and other organizations.

32. A complete text of these standards of care can be obtained through WPATH, on the web at http://www.WPATH.org.

33. Parliament of the World's Religions, *Declaration Toward A Global Ethic*, Chicago, USA, September 4, 1993, Part II, paragraph 7.

34. Wikipedia, *History of Human Rights*, on the web at http://en.wikipedia.org/wiki/Human_rights, as noted on October 15, 2010.

35. United Nations Human Rights Treaties, *International Covenant on Civil and Political Rights*, General Assembly Resolution 2200A of

December 16, 1966, entry into force March 23, 1976.

36. United Nations Human Rights Treaties, *International Covenant on Economic, Social and Cultural Rights*, General Assembly Resolution 2200A of December 1966, entry into force January 3, 1976.

37. Harold Marcuse, Professor of German History, University of California Santa Barbara, this version from the *1997 Poster of Syracuse Culture Workers*, via his web site http://www.history.ucsb.edu/faculty/marcuse/niem.htm.

38. *Webster's New World College Dictionary*, Wiley Publishing, 2007, p. 309.

39. Buscaglia, Leo, *Love, What Life Is All About...*, Fawcett Books, Random House Publishing, ©1972, last printing 1996.

# Glossary of Transgender Terminology

**Introduction.** For transgender people to be understood and ultimately integrated into any culture, a clear and consistent *language* needs to be agreed upon so that we can describe the many aspects of this important and complex phenomenon. Transgender people have historically been so hidden and isolated from their surrounding society and from one another that a common language has been very difficult to establish.

This transgender glossary (including LGBTQ terms) is offered as a reference document that will enable transgender people, family, friends, and professionals of all kinds to better communicate and understand human diversity. Due to the increasing rate of transgender emergence and research, its language will further develop over time. It would be a good idea to refer to the current revision of this glossary regularly on **www.LearnAboutTransgender.org** and **www.TransgenderPortal.com** to keep up to date.

**Androgyne** *n.* A person who lives without appearing or behaving particularly male or female.
**Androgynous** *adj.*, **Androgyny** *n.* Having both masculine and feminine gender typed traits.
**Apparent gender** *n.* The portion of one's socially observable personality that is influenced by or expected from one's assigned sex; the set of publicly displayed gender mannerisms and presentation styles socially categorized as masculine, feminine, androgynous, and neuter.
**Apparent sex** *n.* The anatomical sex that a person appears to be, socially, indicated chiefly by secondary sex characteristics and/or sex-specific clothing.
**Asexual** *adj.* The absence of any sexual attraction.

**Assigned sex** *n.* The anatomical sex applied to people at birth, usually through visual inspection of genitalia.

**Autogynephilia** *n.* In its literal translation means *self-love as a woman*. Diagnostically, autogynephilia is an "erotic obsession with the image of one's self as a woman." Autogynephelia is listed in passing (not as a diagnosis) in the DSM IV. This term caused a fire storm in the transgender community after the release of Michael Bailey's book, "The Man Who Would Be Queen."

**Autosexual** *adj.* Referring to one who's significant sexual activity is masturbation.

**BDSM** An abbreviation for "Bondage, Domination, Sado-Masochism" sexual practices characterized by the consensual exchange of power. This exchange can be either physical (e.g., spanking), psychological (e.g., teasing), or both. Often BDSM involves gender-related play when the partner with power adopts a male role and the partner without power adopts a female role.

**Berdache** *n.* (see Two Spirit). An outdated and now considered derogatory term for "two spirit", a term originating in Native American cultures.

**Bigender** *adj.* 1. describing those who are attracted to both masculine and feminine social genders; the gender equivalent of bisexual. 2. Referring to a person who regularly shifts between masculine and feminine gender expressions, and who does not desire to remain permanently in either. See *Cogender* and *Relational Identity*.

**Bind** *v.* To tape one's breasts flat to the chest to remove their appearance.

**Bisexual, Bi** *adj., n.* One who has significant (to oneself) sexual or romantic attractions to members of both male and female sexes, sometimes including intersex. Contrary to popular myths, people who are attracted to members of more than one sex may be monogamous or non-monogamous (just like people who are attracted only to members of the same sex).

**Blend** *v.* To blend is to present one's chosen gender appropriately enough so as to not draw negative or critical public attention. A more appropriate replacement for the term "pass", which suggests "passing off as" or passing a test. An openly transgender person can *blend* tastefully and successfully

## Glossary of Transgender Terminology

in public in spite of physiological limitations that would make passing virtually impossible, especially under close scrutiny.

**Born (wo)man** *n.* See *genetic (wo)man*. Born (fe)male; may be derogatory.

**Boy** *n.* 1. A young human male. 2. Colloquial term for masculine. Often used to specify the gender of clothes. [I changed into my *boy* clothes.] Boy has often been used as a condescending term for a man (especially a man of color), and is therefore distasteful to many people, except when used in the plural (let's go, boys). (See *girl*.)

**Brain sex** *n.* Referring to the measurable physiological and functional differences between typical (average) male and female brains.

**Butch** *adj., n.* 1. Masculine or macho dress and behavior, regardless of sex or gender identity. 2. A sub-identity of lesbian, gay male, or bisexual, based on masculine or macho dress and behavior. (See *femme*) 3. (*butch it up*) To exaggerate masculine behaviors, usually for others' entertainment. (See *camp*.)

**Camp** *n., adj., vi.* A form of humor, in which one makes fun of one's oppression by taking on and exaggerating stereotypes which the oppressor projects onto the oppressed. Camp makes fun of the stereotype and laughs at the sting of the oppression. Also, *to camp it up*.

**Cisgender** adj. Describing anyone whose social apparent gender aligns naturally with their core gender identity; somewhat the opposite of transgender.

**Cissexual** *adj.* Describing anyone whose socially assigned apparent sex aligns naturally with their core sexual identity; somewhat the opposite of transsexual.

**Clock** *v.* To be perceived by people that one is transsexual or crossdressing. Not passing as the opposite role of that assigned at birth. Being discovered (as in getting a speeding ticket). [I got *clocked* by some teenage girls today.]

**Cogender** *adj.* referring to those who cross-dress in order to express a significant aspect of an inner gender identity. This allows for an ongoing balance between two relatively polarized gender roles: masculine and feminine. A significant change in personality accompanies the change of clothes. (This term is proposed as a more accurate term for either crossdresser or bigender; it indicates two polar genders *co*-existing in the same person, as opposed to the term "bigender" which better describes the mental counterpart to bisexual.)

**Come/be out (of the closet), coming out** *vi*. 1. To disclose one's own inner gender or sexual identity to another person. [I *came out* to my mother over Thanksgiving vacation.] 2. (*to oneself*) To discover that one's own gender or sexual identity is different than one previously assumed; 3. To be open about and deal with one's own and others' reactions to the discovery or disclosure of one's gender or sexual identity. [I am *out* at work.]

**Core identity** *n*. The essential inner sense of self, excluding any social conditioning, comprised of the two aspects *core gender identity* (the part of the whole personality influenced by one's sex) and *core sexual identity* (physiological sense of self).

**Core gender identity** *n*. the portion of one's inner personality that is influenced by one's sexuality, exclusive of any externally applied social conditioning.

**Core sexual identity** *n*. The inner feeling one has regarding one's own physical body, exclusive of any applied social conditioning, especially with regard to one's assigned sex.

**Crossdresser, CD** *n*. A person who temporarily wears clothing typically associated with members of another sex. Most self-defined male crossdressers are heterosexual, distinguishing this group from self-defined drag queens who are usually homosexual or bisexual. Distinguished from the now derogatory and outdated term *transvestite*.

**Crossgender** *adj*. an alternate term for someone living full time in the sex-role other than that assigned at birth, but without GRS. Formerly called *transgender*, which is now an umbrella term. See *trans man, trans woman*.

**Detransition** *n*. To return to living as a member of one's biological sex after an extended full-time period of living as one's target sex.

**Drab** *adj*. Used by MTF crossdressers to describe clothing and appearance

# Glossary of Transgender Terminology 171

of their required gender; opposite of *drag*. Contraction of the phrase DRessed As Boy.

**Drag** *n.* Unusual or dramatic clothing, especially that considered appropriate for another gender.

**Drag King** *n.* A female who presents as male and, often in doing so, purposely takes masculinity to an extreme.

**Drag Queen** *n.* A male who presents as female to an extreme, often for performance purposes. A majority of drag queens are self-defined by their homosexual or bisexual orientation.

**DSM, DSM IV TR** *n.* Abbreviation for the "Diagnostic and Statistical Manual of Mental Disorders" published by the American Psychiatric Association.

**Dyke** *n.* Reclaimed derogatory slang, referring to lesbians or bisexual women, usually more masculine (butch) than femme.

**Dysphoria,** *n.* An emotional state characterized by anxiety, depression or unease. Opposite of euphoria. (see *GID*)

**Electrolysis** *n.* A permanent hair removal process used to eliminate facial and body hair, in this case for gender presentation purposes.

**Female** *n.* One who has strictly the primary sex characteristics of vagina, uterus, ovaries, etc. and no Y chromosome. (Though some persons may appear anatomically female, there are cases where the Y chromosome is present. Technically these persons would be considered intersex.)

**Female impersonator** *n.* A male who dresses and performs so as to appear female, often impersonating celebrity personalities, for entertainment purposes.

**Feminine,** *adj.* **Femininity** *n.* Behavior, thoughts, appearance, and other mannerisms viewed by a culture as typical of females. The gender role assigned to females, typified by nurturing, emotional openness, passiveness, and emphasis on personal appearance.

**Femme** *n., adj.* Feminine or effeminate dress or behavior; a sub-identity of lesbian, gay or bisexual persons based on presentation and behavior.

**Fetish** *n.* Sexual interest in an object not typically viewed as sexual (e.g. boots). Though the term originates as a psychological diagnosis, it is also used in alternative sexuality sub-cultures to refer to a style of dress typified by boots, leather, and latex. For use as a psychological term, one should note that a person can wear fetish attire without having a fetish (e.g., gothic) and one can have a fetish for any object regardless of it's role in a sub-culture (e.g., chalk-boards).

**Fetishistic crossdresser or transvestite** *n.* One who consistently eroticizes crossdressing, possibly with fantasies of changing gender or sex.

**FTM, F2M** *n.* Used to specify the direction of a change in sex or gender: stands for Female To Male or Feminine To Masculine, respectively.

**Gay** *n., adj.* 1. One who has significant (to oneself) sexual or romantic attractions primarily to members of the same sex, or who identifies as a member of the gay community. May be of any gender identity. 2. Sometimes used as a synonym for gay male, lesbian, lesgay, or LesBiGay. Lesbians and Bisexuals often do not feel included by this term.

**Gay community** *n.* 1. The group of people whose members identify as gay. One may identify as gay without identifying as a member of the gay community and vice versa. 2. Sometimes used as a synonym for gay male, lesgay, or LesBiGay community. Lesbians and bisexuals often do not feel included by this term.

**Gender** *n.* A psychological term describing the set of behavioral characteristics that are reserved exclusively for the apparent birth sex of an individual, as determined by the prevailing local culture; that portion of the whole personality that is influenced by one's sex.

**Gender Bend** *v.* To remain within a gender role but push the boundaries by engaging in behavior that is atypical for one's gender (e.g. a girl playing football but still retaining a girlish personality).

**Gender Blend** *v.* To purposely present with strongly visible elements of both sexes (e.g., to have a beard and wear a dress). The intent is typically to provoke people to think about gender roles. Also called Gender Fuck.

**Gender Dysphoria** *n.* A psychiatric term for unhappy or conflicting feelings that can be experienced when one's core gender and/or sexual identity do not match the apparent gender or sexual identity that is socially required by one's assigned birth sex.

## Glossary of Transgender Terminology 173

**Gender Euphoria** *n.* Feeling positive about one's cross-gender activities. The term arises in the transgender community as a pun playing on the psychological term "gender dysphoria"

**Gender Expression** *n.* The external manifestation of one's inner gender identity.

**Gender Fluid** *adj.* referring to a gender identity that changes with time and/or situation as opposed to a fixed sex-role or gender queer expression.

**Gender Identity** *n.* That portion of one's inner personality and values that is influenced by one's sex, exclusive of any social conditioning or suppression. It is distinct from *sexual* identity.

**Gender Identity Disorder, GID** *n.* A psychiatric diagnosis included in the DSM referring to a gender identity that is inconsistent with one's biological sex and/or the social gender role required by it.

**Gender image** *n.* The way one presents oneself to the world, as either male or female.

**Gender orientation** *n.* One's attraction to the gender presentation of another individual, categorized by attraction to the opposite gender, the same gender, both genders or neither gender: heterogender, homogender, bigender or agender, respectively.

**Gender neutral** *adj.* Language that does not use one gender pronoun to represent all people, i.e. does not use "he" and "his" to represent people in general.

**Gender queer** *adj.* See *Queer*.

**Gender Role** *n.* The behaviors, traits, presentation expected by a culture from members of a particular sex; synonymous with sex-role and gender.

**Gender Schema** *n.* A "schema" is an internalized pattern of responses. A gender schema is an internalized pattern of responses that differs by gender. For example, the pattern, "if someone hits me I hit back harder" is characteristic of male gender role behavior.

**Gender Schematic, Gender Aschematic** *adj.* To consider gender an important factor in one's behavior. That is, if you immediately classify a person as male or female and respond to them accordingly, you are gender schematic. Alternatively, if you first classify someone by something other than sex (e.g., race, profession, attractiveness, etc.) and your responses to a person are the same regardless of gender, you are "gender aschematic".

**Genetic, Genetic Male/Female** *n.* Referring to genes and chromosomes, specifically those involved in determining sex. Also meaning classed as such from birth, as in *genetic female* or *genetic male*.

**Genital Reassignment Surgery, GRS** *n.* Formerly termed Sexual Reassignment Surgery (SRS), it is the surgical procedure for changing one's primary sex characteristics from the current (birth) sex to those of one's target sex. Medically these are specifically vaginoplasty for trans women (MTF) and phalloplasty for trans men (FTM).

**GG** *n.* Used mostly by MTF transgender people to refer to someone who is a natal female rather than another trans woman, short for **Genetic Girl**. While some females may find this term demeaning, along with the term "girl," it is not meant as derogatory by transgender people but rather a term of distinction or appreciation.

**Girl** *n.* 1. A young human female. 2. Colloquial term for feminine. Often used for the gender of people or clothes. [I changed into my *girl* clothes.] *Girl* has often been used as a condescending term for a woman, and is therefore distasteful to many people except when used in the plural (let's go, girls). (See *boy*.)

**GLBT**: abbreviation for Gay Lesbian Bisexual Transgender; see *LGBT*.

**Harry Benjamin International Gender Dysphoria Association, HBIGDA** *n.* The original name of the organization of health professionals that maintains the standards of care for the treatment of transsexuals. This organization is now called the World Professional Association for Transgender Health (WPATH).

**Harry Benjamin Standards of Care, HB-SOC, SOC** *n.* A list of rules dictating what is considered by a consensus of health professionals the appropriate way to treat transsexuals; lists available through WPATH.

**Hermaphrodite** *n.* See *Intersex*. 1. An outdated term referring to a person possessing partially expressed genitalia or a combination of the primary and/or secondary sex characteristics of both male or female. Though still used by mental health professionals, those classified as such often consider this term derogatory, instead preferring "intersex" 2. Mythically (almost never happens in reality), one who has both female and male primary and secondary sex characteristics.

**Heterosexual (het)** *n., adj.* 1. Sexual or romantic behavior between a member of one sex and a member of another sex. 2. One whose significant (to oneself) sexual or romantic attractions are primarily to members of another sex. (See *straight*.)

**Homophobia** *n.* 1. An irrational fear of sexual attraction to the same sex or gender. 2. A term for all aspects of the oppression of LesBiGays.

**Homosexual(ity)** *n., adj.* 1. Sexual or romantic behavior between members of the same sex. 2. Formal or clinical term for gay. Homosexual and homosexuality are often associated with the now outdated proposition that same gender attractions are a mental disorder (psychiatric term: homophilia), and are therefore distasteful to some people.

**Hormone Replacement Therapy, HRT** *n.* A therapy of taking sex-related hormones (e.g., estrogen, testosterone). Transgender people undergo HRT to develop the secondary sex characteristics associated with their target sex. This therapy is also used for many post-menopausal women (taking estrogen).

**Humane** *adj.* 1. having what are considered the best qualities of human beings: kind, tender, merciful, sympathetic, etc; 2. without inflicting any more pain than is necessary; 3. with an emphasis on respect for other people's views.

**Identify/ied (as)** *vi.* To hold a particular identity, whether it is a sexual identity, gender identity, national heritage identity (e.g.. Italian), class heritage (e.g. working class), etc. [I *identify* as a woman.] [I am bi *identified*.]

**Identity** *n.* 1. the condition or fact of being a specific person or thing; individuality 2. how one thinks of oneself, as opposed to what others observe or think about one. (See *self-identify, label, gender identity and sexual identity*.)

**In the Life** *adj.* In the African American community, someone who does not fit the traditional gender role assigned to people of their physical sex, either in appearance, behavior, or the gender of a sexual partner.

**Internalized homophobia/biphobia** *n.* The *internalized oppression* of LesBiGay people. This includes the often-conflicting feelings of the internalized homophobic that they are bad at the core; that the entire world is unsafe, that they can only trust other members of their own group; that members of their group are untrustworthy; that for safety they must stay in hiding; that for safety they must come out everywhere, all the time; that their love is bad, or is not the same as other people's love.

**Internalized oppression** *n.* The turning inward and acceptance as true of negative messages and feelings about oneself and one's group, and misinformation about how members of the group (including oneself) deserve to be treated. Internalized oppression often includes messages that contradict one another, as well as messages that reinforce one another.

**International Classes of Diseases, ICD** *n.* An international version of the DSM. Both the DSM and the ICD closely parallel one another.

**Intersex** *adj.* (formerly *Hermaphrodite*) 1. Medically, one who has partially expressed primary or secondary sex characteristics, or a combination of both male and female characteristics. Intersex (pseudo) males are born with a penis, but do not develop most other male secondary sex characteristics such as facial hair, greater muscle density, or sperm with the potential to procreate. Intersex (pseudo) females are born with a vagina, but are often infertile, have more facial hair than most women, and have much lower breast development. There are many forms of intersex physiology involving primary and secondary sex characteristics and chromosomes. Intersex is the preferred term by advocacy groups. 2. One whose external genitalia at birth do not match the standards for male or female (e.g. large clitoris, tiny penis), or one whose sex glands do not totally match the sex assigned at birth (e.g. male with ovarian tissue or female with testicular tissue), or one whose sexual development does not match the sex assigned at birth (e.g. development of penis or extensive facial hair in one assigned as female or the development of breasts in one assigned as male).

**Label** *n.* Name or category applied by someone else, as opposed to self identification.

## Glossary of Transgender Terminology 177

**Lesbian** *n., adj.* A girl or woman who has significant (to oneself) sexual or romantic attractions primarily to members of the same gender or sex, or who identifies as a member of the lesbian community. Bisexual women often do not feel included by this term.

**LesBiGay** *n., adj.* Contraction of "lesbian, bisexual, and gay." Colloquial term for members of sexual orientation minorities. One may identify as LesBiGay without identifying as a member of the LesBiGay community. Usually spelled with capital L, B, G and pronounced with a long "i" to prevent misinterpretation as "only lesbian and gay." Does not include the transgender community.

**LGBT(Q)** *adj.* The acronym for Lesbian Gay Bisexual Transgender, referring to organizations and services seeking support of these groups who share in discrimination, loss of civil rights, and similar health needs. The acronym LGBTQ also exists, the Q referring to Queer (gender queer) or Questioning. Sometimes stated as GLBT or GLBTQ.

**Lifestyle choice** *n.* The incorrect assumption that one's gender and sexual identities and orientations are chosen through experimentation rather than being formed before rational development.

**Lipstick lesbian** *n.,* A femme lesbian, characterized by the very feminine presentations such as make-up, clothing and mannerisms.

**Male** *n.* One who has only the primary sex characteristics of normally a penis and testicles, and the Y chromosome.

**Male impersonator** *n.* A female who, on specific occasions, assumes the appearance, voice, and often extreme mannerisms of a male, for entertainment purposes.

**Man** *n.* The social role of a male, not to be confused with the term "male". Man is the sex-role of a male.

**Masculine,** *adj.,* **Masculinity** *n.* Behaviors, thoughts, appearance, and other mannerisms viewed by a culture as typical of males. The gender role assigned to males, typified by strength, assertiveness, athleticism, emotional containment.

**Monosexual** *n., adj.* One who has significant sexual or romantic attractions only to members of one gender or sex. Straight, gay, lesbian. Not bisexual or asexual. Regarded as derogatory and offensive by some, especially gay men and lesbians.

**Monosexism/ist** *n.* A particular subset of the oppression of bisexuals. The assumption that one can (or should) be attracted to members of only one sex, and that having sexual or romantic attractions to more than one gender/sex is bad and unacceptable.

**MTF, M2F** *adj.* Used to specify the direction of a change in sex or gender: stands for Male To Female or Masculine To Feminine, respectively.

**Neuter** *adj.* 1. Referring to one who has neither female nor male primary sex characteristics. 2. Occasionally used to mean androgynous.

**Non-op transsexual** *n.* One who thinks of oneself as transsexual (sexual identity as opposed to gender identity) and lives in the role of their self-identified sex but is unable to undergo GRS or is not satisfied with the potential results. For example many FTM people (trans men) would not be satisfied with the results that phalloplasty surgery (construction of a penis) would produce, and choose not to exchange the genitals they were born with for an unsatisfactory version of the other. Other transsexuals have financial or health issues that prevent desired surgery. Some people already in a relationship choose to remain in that relationship and retain the sex organs from their birth, even though they identify as the opposite sex. Non-op transsexuals crossdress and undergo hormone therapy and (if MTF) electrolysis to modify secondary sex characteristics.

**Normal** *n.* average; often biased to mean "right," "acceptable," "proper."

**Oppositional sexism** *n.* A social perspective that defines the male and female sexes as having little or nothing in common; that males and females are mutually exclusive.

**Orchiectomy** *n.* The removal of the testes; the medical term for castration. Some trans women have an "orchie" to stop the production of testosterone, or in lieu of GRS that may be either in the distant future or not possible.

**Out** *n.* Having (had) public disclosure of one's inner gender or sexual identity. (See *come out*.)

**Out, outing** *vt.* 1. To disclose a second person's inner and private gender or sexual identity to a third person, especially without the second person's permission. 2. To disclose one's own gender or sexual identity, often without intending or choosing to do so. [I *outed* myself by leaving a political letter on my desk, which my boss saw when he was looking for me.] (See *come out*.) 3. To reveal that a person now living in a new sex-role is in fact transgender when this fact is not desired to be publicly known.

**Pack** *v.* To put an object, often a dildo, in one's pants to suggest to others the presence of a penis.

**Pansexual** *adj.* Referring to those who desire an intimate relationship with persons expressing a variety of different gender and/or sexual identities; not confined to the attraction of just a single sex or gender category.

**Paraphilia** *n.* A sex-drive directed at any non-socially accepted object or activity. Kissing, though directed at an object not directly linked to procreation, is not considered a paraphilia because it is socially acceptable. A fetish is a kind of paraphilia. Transgender expression is currently considered a paraphilia but homosexuality no longer is.

**Pass, Passing** *v.* To succeed at being perceived as one's target sex, i.e. as a man or a woman, contrary to one's birth sex. (see *blend*)

**Ping** *v.* To scrutinize a person in order to ascertain whether they are transgender or not (as in a sonar ping) [I'm being *pinged* by that man].

**Polyamorous** *adj.* Having multiple intimate relationships concurrently; similar to polygamous but without formal commitment.

**Post-Operative** *adj.*, **Post-Op (Transsexual)** *n.* A transsexual man or woman who has completed GRS, formerly called SRS.

**Pre-Operative** *adj.* **Pre-Op (Transsexual)** *n.* A transsexual man or woman who is planning but has not yet had GRS, due to Real Life Experience requirements, financial restrictions, health, or other issues.

**Present** *v.* To appear as one's chosen gender. That is, to *present* as female or feminine means to look and behave in a manner to be viewed by others as female.

**Primary Sex Characteristics** *n.* The genitalia associated with each sex, inclusively for males the penis, prostate and testicles, and for females the clitoris, vagina, uterus and ovaries.

**Primary Transsexual** *n.* Originally a mental health term referring to a transsexual who seeks GRS during adolescence or emerging adulthood. The classification is no longer viewed as important for the mental health community.

**Purge** *v.* Throwing away or destroying of one's clothes and effects of another ("the opposite") sex, usually driven by feelings of guilt. Often part of a cycle of yielding to gender expression, then rejecting it out of guilt, and so on.

**Queer** *n.* Deviation from societal norms for gender and/or sexual behavior. A formerly derogatory slang for the homosexual minority. Queer is an umbrella term of empowerment to many younger gender-variant and sexual-variant sub-groups to mean different, non-conforming, outside the mainstream.

**Queer spawn** *n.* Children of transgender/gender queer parent(s), self applied by these offspring.

**Radical Feminism** *n.* A branch of feminism that was particularly popular among "second-wave feminists" in the 1960's. It advocates a post-modern perspective and views sex groups (males & females) as social classes. Many cultures are patriarchal, where the male social class controls the female social class. When SRS first became readily available, radical feminists opposed transsexuality. This is a belief that is not often shared by those in generation X, third-wave feminism.

**Read** 1. *v.i.* To have been discovered as a member of one's birth sex despite presenting as a member of one's target sex. The failure to pass or blend as one's preferred gender [I've been *read* by that teenager]. Other slang synonyms are "clocked", "made". 2. *vt.* To discover another's true sex in spite of their presenting as the other.

**Real Life Test (RLT) or Real Life Experience (RLE)** *n.* A requirement of the International Standards of Care that transsexuals live for a minimum of one year full time as their target sex before GRS. The most recent ISOC renamed the real life test as "real life experience" though it still retains it's test-like use.

**Relational Identity** *n.* The nature of one's attraction to other people, comprised of Gender Orientation (attraction to the gender part of

## Glossary of Transgender Terminology 181

personality) and Sexual Orientation (attraction to sex characteristics).

**Same gender/sex** *n., adj.* 1. The same gender or sex as the reference person's own. [My partner is same sex.] 2. Two or more people of the same gender or sex. [I met another *same gender* couple at church today.]

**Same-gender attraction** n. The gender counterpart to homosexual: being attracted to the same gender regardless of genitalia. Since attraction involves both sexual and gender identities, it is appropriate to distinguish gender orientation from sexual orientation.

**Secondary Sex Characteristics** *n.* Anatomical traits linked to biological sex but not directly involved in procreation (e.g., breasts, facial hair).

**Secondary Transsexual** *n.* Originally a mental health term referring to a transsexual who seeks GRS in middle adulthood. The classification is no longer viewed as important for the mental health community.

**Self-identify** *v.*, **self-identity** *n.* One's internal sense of self, as opposed to external or social expectations or interpretations of it.

**Sex** *n.* 1. The biological condition of being male, female, intersex, or neuter, as determined by chromosomes and primary sex characteristics. 2. The act of sexual intimacy or intercourse.

**Sex-role** *n.* The behavioral and appearance requirements defined by a prevailing culture based upon one's sex as assigned at birth (synonymous with gender role and gender).

**Sexual Identity** *n.* How one thinks of oneself anatomically, based on internal experience as opposed to external norms, expectations or actual physiology. It is distinct from gender identity.

**Sexuality** *n.* 1. the instincts, drives, behavior, etc. associated with one's anatomical sex 2. of, characteristic of, or involving sex, the sexes, the organs of sex and their functions.

**Sexual Minority** *n. adj.* Used variously to refer to members of the LGBTQ community. The term is currently in flux and may vary considerably by region and specific community.

**Sexual orientation** *n.* The physical attraction to another's anatomical sex characteristics, categorized by attraction to either another sex, the same sex, both male and female sexes, or no sex: heterosexual, homosexual, bisexual or asexual respectively.

**Sexual preference** n. What a person likes to do (prefers) in sexual interaction. It is a conscious recognition or choice not to be confused with sexual orientation. *Sexual preference* emphasizes that some people feel that one does or should have some control or influence over the development of one's sexual identity.

**Sexual Reassignment Surgery, SRS** *n.* Outdated term for the surgical procedure for changing one's primary sex characteristics from the current (birth) sex to those of one's target sex. Medically these are specifically vaginoplasty for trans women and phalloplasty for trans men. Now termed Genital Reassignment Surgery (GRS).

**She-Male** *n.* Used by the pornography industry to refer to generally non-op or pre-op transsexual women with penises, emphasizing the fact that while appearing to be women in other regards, they most definitely do have a penis. Derogatory term, reclaimed by some people.

**Sissy Boy** *n.* A term codified by the mental health community for biologically male children with gender identity disorder.

**Stealth, woodworking** *adj.* A mode in which a post-transition trans man or trans woman conceals his or her past sex.

**Stone Butch** *n.* A lesbian who exhibits strong male gender (masculine) behavior, especially including emotion control. The term arises from Leslie Fineberg's book "Stone Butch Blues"

**Straight** *n., adj.* Colloquial for heterosexual. *Straight* has connotations of "unadulterated," "pure," and "honest," and some members of the sexual identity community find distasteful the implication that one who is not straight is "bent," "adulterated," "impure," or "dishonest." *Straight* also has connotations of "narrow," "straight-laced" or "conservative," and some heterosexual people find that distasteful. Alternate spellings: strait, strayt, str8.

**Target Sex** *n.* The desired sex or sex-role of a transsexual or transgender person, as opposed to one's current biological or assigned sex.

**T-friendly** *adj.* Any organization or institution that is accepting of transgender people and their needs.

# Glossary of Transgender Terminology

**Transbian** *n.* Slang for a male-to-female (MTF) transsexual who identifies as lesbian.

**Transexual** *adj.* Purposely spelled with only one "s", this term was intended to take the psychological term from the mental health professional sub-culture and re-define it for the transgender sub-culture.

**Transgender** *adj.* An umbrella term referring to any person who regularly feels and may consequently desire to act and/or appear significantly inconsistent with the social sex-role requirements or restrictions established by the prevailing local culture. Transgender identity can be expressed through any combination of personal appearance (clothing and adornment), behavior (personality and mannerisms), or anatomy.

**Transition** *n.* The process of openly switching from one's birth sex and/or gender to one's target sex and/or gender. Transitioning has many phases, but many feel it is life-long.

**Trans man** *n.* An openly transgender man. This term is either self-applied or used by others with consent. Since it does not specify any anatomical information, such as the term *transsexual* does, it is often preferred by openly transgender FTM people (see *trans woman*).

**Transphobia** *n.*, **transphobic** *adj.* The fear and hatred of crossdressers, transsexuals and gender benders and what they do (or are feared to do). This ranges from disrespect, to denial of rights and needs, to violence. A form of oppression based on gender identity expression.

**Transsexual (TS)** *n., adj.* One who desires to change one's primary and secondary sex characteristics to align these with one's core sexual identity. The change of primary sex characteristics is accomplished by GRS (SRS), while secondary characteristics are achieved through a combination of hormone therapy, electrolysis, facial feminization surgery (FFS), breast reduction or augmentation, and other treatments or procedures. Since surgery is not a defining factor of being transgender, the term transsexual is applied only to those who publicly define themselves as such. Sometimes spelled *transexual*. (See *pre-op TS, non-op TS, trans man/woman*)

**Transvestite (TV)** *n.* A historically psycho-pathological term that refers to one who mainly crossdresses for pleasure in the appearance and sensation.

The pleasure may be erotic (see *fetishistic transvestite*), empowering, rebellious or something else. May feel comfortable in the corresponding gender role while crossdressed. May occasionally experience gender dysphoria. May be of any gender identity. In the UK this term has been synonymous with *crossdresser*.

**Trans woman** *n.* An openly transgender woman. This term is either self-applied or used by others with consent. Since it does not specify any anatomical information, such as the term *transsexual* does, it is often preferred by openly transgender MTF people (see *trans man*).

**TS** *n.* Short for transsexual.

**Tuck** *v.* To tape one's penis and testicles back to remove the suggestion of their presence.

**Two Spirit** *adj.* In some Native American tribes, this refers to people who did not fit the traditional gender role (through their behavior, or activities, or the sex of their partner) usually assigned to their physical sex. Depending on the tribe, they might fit into a different accepted sex-role, or be regarded as religious leaders, or they might simply choose to live in the gender role usually assigned to another physical sex. The French term *berdache*, meaning mattress, has been widely used by anthropologists, but is now considered a derogatory cultural imposition.

**Unisex** *adj.* Clothing, behaviors, thoughts, feelings, relationships, etc. that are considered appropriate for members of both genders/sexes. (See *gender neutral*.)

**Woman** *n.* 1. The social sex-role of a female, not to be confused with the term female. Woman is behavioral, female is anatomical. 2. One who identifies with the feminine gender role of a female, regardless of present sex or sexual identity. Plural: women, wymyn, wimmin.

**Womyn, wymyn** *n.* Feminist spelling of the terms *woman* and *women* respectively *(specifically to exclude the syllables "man" and "men")*.

**Woodworking** *adj.*, see *stealth*.

© 2010 Claire Ruth Winter

# About the Author

Claire Ruth Winter was born male, Lawrence Winter, and at the age of 3 began a lifelong struggle with strong and confusing inner feelings that we now recognize as *gender dysphoria* (at that time thought to be sexual perversion). During childhood his father's medical career took the family to live in such places as American Samoa, Alaska, Hawaii, and the continental U.S., giving him valuable exposure to cultural and racial diversity.

He graduated from Whitman College, ranked in the top 50 colleges and universities in the U.S., with a BA degree in music education and a minor in math/physics. He combined these and eventually cofounded a successful commercial audio electronics manufacturing corporation with worldwide distribution, where he developed product design concepts, print ads, brochures, manuals and traveled extensively to provide training and education.

Lacking the educational and internet resources of today, he was unable to pinpoint the nature of his lifelong gender struggle until 1986, when television and print media began to more intelligently explore transgender issues. A newly discovered real, though part-time, inner identity he named Claire soon became very active in local and national transgender organizations: serving on boards, publishing newsletters, writing educational pamphlets and attending national conferences—by necessity in complete stealth from family, friends and colleagues.

He eventually sold his interest in his corporation and, realizing his true and whole identity to be Claire, she began her transition to become legally female, during which she started a new career as a full-time transgender educator and author.

Ms. Winter has been an active member of many advocacy organizations including the ACLU, COLAGE, Gender Odyssey, the International Foundation for Gender Education (IFGE), the National Center for Transgender Equality (NCTE), The Task Force, Trans

186    Understanding Transgender Diversity

Youth Family Advocates (TYFA), the Washington Transgender Equality Project (WATEP), and others.

She created and maintains the public educational web sites **www.LearnAboutTransgender.org** and **www.TransgenderPortal.com**, has written many educational pamphlets and articles, and lectures to college and university undergraduate and graduate classes and transgender conferences. She lives in her home of 35 years, in the countryside near Duvall, Washington, where she raised her son with whom she remains very close.

2008 with son Shane.

2003 before transition.

2009

Photo: HumaNature 2009